MEN THE HANDBOOK

MEN
THE HANDBOOK

MINDI RUDAN

COOL HAND COMMUNICATIONS, INC.
BOCA RATON, FLORIDA

Copyright ©1995 by Mindi Rudan

ISBN: 1-56790-113-1

First Printing

All rights reserved. No part of this book may be reproduced by any means without the express written permission of the publisher.

COOL HAND COMMUNICATIONS, INC.
1098 N.W. Boca Raton Boulevard, Suite 1
Boca Raton, FL 33432

Printed in the United States of America

Book design by Cheryl Nathan

Front cover photos from top to bottom: Marina Larenz, Sheila K. Harlin, Vicky Vassallo, Norweign Cruise Line

Back cover photos from top to bottom: The Test Board, Inc., Marina Larenz, Terry Boykin, Paula Norton

Rudan, Mindi
    Men, the handbook / Mindi Rudan.
       p.   cm.
    ISBN 1-56790-113-1
    1. Men--United States--Psychology--Case studies. 2. Man-woman relationships--United States--Case studies. 3. Interpersonal relations--United States--Case studies. I. Title.
    HQ1090.3.R83 1994
    305.31--dc20   94-37342
                                                                      CIP

Dedication

To my two best friends:
my husband, Hank, and "Lynn" (Lorraine), my mom,
for infusing me with God's most precious gift ...
unconditional love.

In remembrance of my "gramma" Rose and "poppa" Dave,
for their old world wit and wisdom.

In memory of my Dad, "Rip" (Maurice),
for your class, dignity and kindness. I didn't have much time
to tell you, but I hope the person I strive to be is your legacy.

To my brother Alan, the teacher,
for not kicking my butt when you got older and "coulda"
and for being my friend.

Acknowledgements

My heartfelt thanks to my dear friend, writer/editor Nina L. Diamond (who's single), for being an unending source of material and immeasurable encouragement. You were always available to me when I needed you, even if you did call me a twit a few zillion times.

To Chris, Maddie, Hans, Pete, Kim, Cheryl and Lisa at Cool Hand Communications for being a wonderful team and publishing this book in record time.

To the thousands of women who have written me over the years and who prompted this book. I care about your lives, and I hope this book proves that, by making things a little clearer and a little easier.

And to the almost 4,000 men I have interviewed and spoken to in the last four years—you opened up your hearts and souls to make this book possible. You openly gave me a depth of understanding and insight afforded very few. I hope this book did you justice.

Contents

Preface		iii
Introduction		1
Part One	**Back To The Beginning**	5
Chapter 1	The New Definition Of "Single"	7
Part Two	**Successfully Single**	11
Chapter 2	Alice In Wonderland Or Alice In Purgatory? Exploring Your Own Definition Of Single	13
Chapter 3	Living Happily Ever After ... Even *Before* Marriage	19
Chapter 4	Understanding What Is Happening To Men In The '90s	25
Chapter 5	Successfully Single — Embarking On The Journey	31
Part Three	**How To Meet A Man**	35
Chapter 6	Man Finding — Let me Count The Ways	37
Chapter 7	The Resource Directory — Clubs, Groups, And Organizations To Help Your Ying Find Its Yang	55
Chapter 8	Being Who You Really Are	69
Chapter 9	"A" You're Adorable, "B" You're So Beautiful— The Key To Unlocking Your Desirability	73
Chapter 10	The First Date— Wisdom To Make Sure There's A Second	90
Chapter 11	Dating Do's & Dating Don'ts— A Practical Guide	99
Part Four	**How To Marry A Man— Secrets For Moving The Relationship Up To The Next Level**	109
Chapter 12	The "Why Factor" And How To Apply It In Your Own Relationships	110
Chapter 13	Determining Lifestyle Compatibility	121
Chapter 14	Monkey See, Monkey Do— How Our Parents' Relationships Impact Our Own	126
Chapter 15	Expectations— Identifying Yours and Sorting Reality From Fantasy	130
Chapter 16	Expectations Are Like Lips: Everyone Has Them. It's What You Do With Them That Counts	133
Chapter 17	How To Choose Who's Right And Avoid Who's Wrong	138
Chapter 18	Closeness and Commitment: The Truth About How Men *Really* Feel	157
Part Five	**How To Mature With A Man**	183
Chapter 19	He Said, She Thought— The Secrets For Compassionate Communication Between The Sexes	184
Chapter 20	Romance—What It Is And What It Is Not	205
Chapter 21	Love Is The Answer— How To Keep The Bonfires Burning ... Forever	216
Epilogue		233

Preface

For years, women have tried to unlock the mystery of what men actually think about relationships, love and commitment, and searching for an omniscient crystal ball that reveals these answers, resembles Monty Python's pursuit of the Holy Grail.

We say we want to know, but do we really? Do we genuinely want to understand what makes men withdraw? Do we actually want to hear why they hide their emotions from us or understand their responses to *our* emotions? Or will the truth make us flinch?

Hundreds of interpretative books have been written by psychologists, human relations experts and therapists, all claiming to *know* how men think. Many more have been written on how to *land* a man and how to make love to a man and keep him from straying. Women have devoured these books, yet the discord and confusion remain. Why? Because somewhere along the line we forgot to simply *ask* how the real man actually feels. After all, the idea of the totally non-verbal male icon may just not be apropos in describing *today's* modern male.

From my thousands of *Bachelor Book* interviews, it is clear that men today feel like test cultures in a laboratory—being poked and prodded, bisected and dissected. If only that brain in formaldehyde could talk!

It can't, but *men can*... and in MEN: The Handbook, real men *did talk*, speaking out openly and honestly, sharing their innermost thoughts. From Fortune 500 company CEO's to local postmen, to hundreds upon hundreds of men in between, they spilled their guts, exposing their vulnerabilities, their confusions and sometimes, their anger.

MEN: The Handbook will give you insight into men like no book ever has before, but some women may not enjoy reading the text because its premise points no fingers, and presumes no blame.

MEN: The Handbook infuses both men and women with the information needed to share in the responsibility of causing relationship rifts, and therefore helps the readers to heal each other. This kind of message may upset some women, who may, in turn, wish to silence me—the messenger. But in this book, the men are speaking to you directly, you owe it to yourself to at least listen to them.

Introduction

Through the years as editor, publisher, interviewer and resident rent-a-shoulder for *the BACHELOR BOOK*, a national magazine profiling hundreds of single, eligible men genuinely seeking relationships, I have been afforded a vantage point to which few are privy. Exposed to the very hearts and souls of single people everywhere, I have been Mother Confessor, friend and committed listener to thousands of single men and, through them, single women. The information they have shared with me has been straight from the heart, always frank, often startling and unquestionably eye-opening.

MEN: The Handbook is the synthesis of these interviews, painstakingly gleaned and organized; drawn directly from what men of all ages, income brackets, ethnic backgrounds and all walks of life have confided to me. *MEN: The Handbook* is the breakthrough that will facilitate constructive communication, real compassion and educated understanding between the genders. It is the key that, used properly, unlocks the door to successfully establishing healthy, nurturing, give-and-take relationships—*that have the power to last*. The thousands of men interviewed for this book have shared their innermost thoughts, their needs, their dreams, their disappointments, their hurts, wants, insecurities and also their expectations. They've candidly talked about the women with whom they've been involved and those they'd dream of having a relationship with. Openly and honestly they've detailed what they admire in women and what they don't. With great pains they describe their confusion and fears with respect to the new rules, changing roles and changing demands which *they feel* seem to be made upon them daily giving insight into how that makes them feel, and therefore why they *react* as they do—priceless information, imperative if women are to relate to men *successfully*.

I have sorted and organized the thousands of questions I have been asked time and time again, and have isolated the major problems, roadblocks and pitfalls both men and women encounter in establishing long-term fulfilling relationships, and have offered concrete solutions to avoid much of the confusion. But, most importantly, what this book does is not just clarify circumstance and offer abatement; *MEN: The Handbook* unravels the reasons *behind* the confusion.

I have always been the kind of person who needed to understand the *why* behind the question, rather than just be given the answer to it. If I understand why something happened, I have opportunity to work it out correctly the next time, and the time after that. If I never learn which wire connects to which terminal, I'll need *the same* help over and over, which is stagnating. And while it's unrealistic to expect to be a jack of all trades when our possessions go on the blink, it's an entirely different matter in our personal lives. Caring, thinking, feeling, loving and intelligent people must at least make an attempt to understand how to successfully build a lasting bond with a partner. Finding and keeping true love is one of the most pervasive and important goals in everyone's life. Isn't it worth a little extra time to understand the dynamics before attempting to solve the equation?

The times when I've felt the most helpless, not to mention hopeless, have been when I didn't understand the *why* behind something.

MEN: The Handbook introduces what I have come to call the "Why Factor," that all-important bit of knowledge needed to process information *correctly*. Information that up to now has been missing to assess relationships *accurately*. I believe this book will clear up common and not so common misunderstandings, miscommunications, and cultural and gender-related misconceptions. It does so by sharing the incredible insights gained from talking *directly* to thousands of men who all genuinely seek healthy, long-term, monogamous relationships and fusing that information with concrete evidence gleaned from various studies, explaining how we got here in the first place and how many of the deeply ingrained feelings which overtake us are derived from an ancient gene pool, causing confusion as to why we act and feel the way we do.

MEN: The Handbook will help you understand.

I have written this book as sincerely and genuinely as I know how. I care very deeply for the single men and women I see searching for that special someone and have written this book to share the vast amount of information I have absorbed over the years. I'm offering the information I've learned with my heart, with my level head and with the stubborn streak that has always propelled me to ferret out the truth and separate it from fiction. I hope this book will teach you about men in a way you've never been taught before; learning how to understand the way men think and process information, and how to correctly decipher many of the *reasons* behind what causes them to react as they do. I sincerely hope this book is the catalyst that leads you towards the healthy, monogamous, lasting love that you desire; enabling you to treat not just the opposite sex with more understanding and compassion, but *everyone*.

Part One
Back To The Beginning

Chapter 1: The New Definition Of "Single"

Just what does being *single* mean today? Mr. Webster defines it as: "unmarried." Mrs. Webster says it's "what your boyfriend of one year better not refer to himself as."

Being single today is not like being single in any other time in our culture's history. It means rethinking almost every aspect of your life. We used to bemoan the status quo; today there is none.

The single years used to bridge being part of a family and then creating one of your own. As values changed, so did the so called rules on being single and dating.

No longer the innocent '50s or the rebellious '60s, or the free-love '70s, or the "me" era '80s. In the '90s, apparently there are no concrete rules. The times, indeed, have changed. A recent quote from Ike, the bartender on the TV show "Love and War" sums it up best: "Today I serve men in ponytails sending drinks to women in crewcuts." Being single in the '90s when almost 42% of the adult population of the United States is also unattached is, to say the least, quite different. And perhaps more importantly, of the 85 million adults who find themselves single now, in this era of AIDS, 900 numbers, personals and video dating, many only had prior dating experience in one of those bygone eras! What worked twenty years ago has changed drastically today. Women and men are caught up in a flurry of changing roles and expectations. "Should I open my own door or should I let him?" "Do I grab the check or will she think I'm sexist?" One of the reasons dating in the '90s is so different from any other era is simply the sheer number of singles. With the divorce rate above 50%, the new definition of "single" suggests a diversity and complexity unmatched in the history of our culture. No longer is this group represented solely by young singles making their first solo flight from the nest just prior to marriage, nor the widowed elderly who have lost a spouse after a lifetime of marriage—the two basic groups that primarily constituted "singles" back in the 1950s. In the 1990s, singles span every age group, income level, ethnic background and life-style. Encompassing young men and women single-handedly raising one, two or more children, this group is often plagued with guilt, frustration, time restraints and logistical problems no one ever told them they'd face. Raising kids in a two parent household is hard enough, going it alone and trying to find the time to meet a new mate becomes next to impossible. Years ago, dad almost always was the "child-free" parent, concerned only with the weekend or holiday visit. How often did we hear of a father retaining or seeking *custody* fifteen or even ten years ago? Infrequent at best. He was the one who often remarried first, being unencumbered and without the same worries, time restraints and monetary concerns as the custodial parent.

Today, as fathers relish their equal rights and responsibilities, both genders face such dilemmas, and so does the unencumbered single who enters into a relationship with a single parent.

"Single" now also includes women and men in their forties and fifties, raising young children or teenagers. "Single" can mean "empty nesters" in almost any age category, who find themselves completely alone, many for the first time. With no kids, no spouse, and no earthly idea how to be single now. The last time many of *these* men and women were single was maybe fifteen, twenty or even twenty-five years ago. Remember back then, when you took a car trip with the family and could identify almost every other car on the road? Try that now. That's reflective for those men and women who were single in the '50s and '60s and are now reentering the dating scene after a prolonged absence. Like Rip Van Winkle waking after a twenty year sleep, they must be scratching their collective heads wondering, *What the hell happened while I was gone?*

Also mixed into this convoluted cauldron is an entirely new phenomenon: the professional. In their mid thirties to forties, these are the folks who intentionally delayed marriage in favor of establishing a career. Years ago women in this category were called "spinsters" or "old-maids." As the terms have changed, so have the perceptions. Today, women in this category are highly desirable, powerful, intelligent, independent and focused. Able to leap tall buildings in a single bound and willing to postpone personal satisfaction for professional achievement. Indeed, these are accomplished, distinguished individuals who, when it comes to dating, find themselves as naive as a kindergartner on his or her first day of school. They also find themselves, somewhat to their chagrin, much more discriminating than they were ten years ago. The tanned, muscle-bound lifeguard who caught their eye at twenty, is a far cry from the man whom they envision themselves making a life with at forty. This group discovers that simply picking up their social life where they left it, isn't as simple as they thought it would be. On the contrary, in the years they concentrated on building careers and a secure foundation for their lives, dating became a veritable mine field of unsuitable suitors. And then, as powerful and secure as this group perceives themselves to be... one question from a Jewish or Italian mother can topple them to their knees like a banana tree cut down in its prime by a machete: "So, Wonder Woman, when do you think you're going to finally find some time to make me a grandmother?"

Some perceptions die harder than others.

Add to the new definition of single the group that chooses to remain child-free, those not looking for a ready-made family or any family for that matter, and those who are. Then incorporate into this picture, the newest dimension to singledom, the less overt but still vibrant "senior singles" in their late fifties to seventies. These folks aren't yet ready to hang up their sneakers and be relegated to being simply grandpa and grandma the baby-sitter. With the extension of life expectancy and our society's emphasis on health and prolonging youth, this group is younger in body, mind and spirit than ever before. They've entered the arena en masse and they too, are looking for viable partners, but very different kinds of partners than their younger counterparts. Paul Newman, as he enters his seventies is as sexy and charismatic as ever. This guy is certainly *not* ready for a blanket and rocking chair. Joan Rivers is more attractive than she ever was, and she's now sixty-plus with a career in full blast and much younger suitors in lust! Ted Turner and Jane Fonda found a deep, abiding love in their mid-fifties. As deep and profound, perhaps even more so, than you're able to uncover in your twenties.

It's clear that being single today has many faces.

But how does each of these very different groups of singles find fulfilling companionship? And is the definition of fulfillment different as you move from one group to another? What category do you fit into and where do you find your own group of contemporaries? What are the parameters today? And how does a man's age, upbringing and thoughts on our changing society affect his behavior within a relationship? Read on, and you'll find the answers to these questions and more as you come closer to identifying who you are, where you fit in, what your expectations are, how to successfully match them to someone who shares your direction, and how to *sustain* that love once you find it.

Part Two
Successfully Single

Chapter 2

Alice In Wonderland Or Alice In Purgatory?

Exploring Your Own Definition Of Single

During a speaking engagement in Chicago, Laurie, a young woman of about thirty listened to my presentation and then approached me as I was preparing to leave. "I hate being single," she said to me. "I hated it the first time, and here I am floundering in the midst of it again."

As tired and anxious as I was to get back to my hotel and kick off the miniature torture chambers they call high heels, I could clearly see she needed to talk, and invited her to walk with me, or more accurately *hobble* with me, out to the waiting car.

"What didn't you like about being single the first time?" I asked.

"Everyone looking at me like there was something wrong with me if I didn't have a man. Feeling like I was half a person if I wasn't part of a couple," she replied. "I joined clubs, went on countless blind dates. I did everything the books tell you to do. I went at it like a business and then I met Nick."

I'll cut to the chase: Nick turned out to be a handsome, articulate albeit rather boorish, self-centered, the world-revolves-around-me type who, after eight years of marriage, spied someone he thought would make the world spin faster for him. After a wee bit of prodding, Laurie admitted she knew from the very start, that Nick was less than her ideal match.

"He was good-looking, had a decent job, and I was really tired of running around looking for Mr. Right," she said.

I could have finished the story for her. There are thousands upon thousands of singles who "settle" for a relationship because they're tired of being alone, tired of fielding the *Why don't you have a mate* question and tired of spending yet another waking moment listening intently to a story spewed by a member of the opposite sex whom they couldn't care less about.

It all comes down to the question of how you perceive being single. Laurie is an example of a woman who views her single years as though she's serving a sentence for a crime she didn't commit. Consciously, she was choosing a man she hoped would be her life partner. Unconsciously, she was justifying her worth. She hoped they'd grow together and that love would conquer whatever was missing in the relationship. Nick was her "get-out-of-jail-free" card.

When I was a guest on a local talk show in Milwaukee several years ago, a beautiful woman in her mid forties stood up and asked me on-camera why her first husband watched only sports, went bowling, played cards, but had no desire to share even one of her interests, and then she ended up marrying another man just like him? "I thought that when I got married the second time we'd learn new hobbies, share interests and explore new adventures together," she said.

It's hard to understand and solve someone's problems in the forty seconds a talk show allows you to be brilliant, but after the show I sat with her, pen and paper in hand, taking notes. It seems she had a somewhat overbearing mother and couldn't wait to get out of the house. The family wasn't overly affluent, so college wasn't an option. Marriage was. "Have you ever been single and on your own?" I asked.

"Only the eleven months between the time I left my first husband and moved in with the second."

"What did you do with that time?" I asked.

"What do you mean?" came the perplexed reply.

"Did you use any of that time to enjoy yourself, learn more about yourself, to travel or experience some of the things you always wanted to try?" I asked.

"No," she said, as she began to turn the color of white zinfandel, "I concentrated on finding another husband."

I could go on with the conversation, and actually cite hundreds more that were almost identical, but I think the point I'm about to make is already taking shape. Despite the opportunities afforded women when they're single, very few take advantage of them, viewing the "single life" instead as a time they merely survive while focusing on eventual marriage. They view it as purgatory, a sort of nothingness, a mere stopgap. The notion that we could learn to be happy, productive individuals whether or not we're married, seems unbelievable to most. And it's not our fault; society has skewed women in that direction while training men on an entirely different, however, parallel track.

"I had a great time when I was single," lamented a rugged, recently divorced, just-turned-fifty airline pilot from Washington state, who attended one of my seminars. "When I was single and just starting my career, I had a ball. I met hundreds of women and I really got a chance to sow my wild oats. I remember it took some fancy foot work, but I managed to stay 'unhooked' until thirty-one."

Apparently someone must have left the cage door open again, because he was on the prowl with the same misguided biases he had as a young single—believing that every female he comes in contact with is looking to put a ring through his nose. And it isn't so much his fault either. Here's where understanding the origins of these feelings becomes so relevant.

The idea of romantic love is a concept that historically went against the grain. Why does the tragic love affair of Romeo and Juliet symbolize the heart and soul of lovers everywhere down through the ages? Because their *romantic love* was taboo in a world that coupled for economic or political gain. Historically, marriages and couplings were fulfilled first by the human race's basic need for survival in primitive society. Since the female bore the children and would then have to nurse and nurture them, men were looked upon as a necessity for survival. Not only did they have to hunt food, they had to protect the female from danger. Later, marriages were arranged for familial gain in preindustrial society. Empires were created, dynasties perpetuated, even business benefited by the "right" marriage. Just forty years ago, in the pre-Women's Movement days, a woman's ultimate position in life was determined solely by the kind of man she wed. "You'll grow up sweetheart, and marry a doctor," was the hope of most mothers. Until she took a husband, a woman's life was viewed as incomplete. Is it any wonder most contemporary women were brought up viewing singledom as akin to the bubonic plague? While men on the other hand, were instructed to "sow their wild oats, get things out of their systems, experience life and the world" before they became saddled with the "old ball and chain, and all the baby bawls." Following that train of thought, is it difficult to see why many modern men may feel they are being ensnared even if you personally have done nothing to cause those feelings to surface?

The idea of romantic love, of a person freely choosing the mate he or she desires, is a relatively new concept. The Greeks didn't believe in marrying for love, the poet Pallatas stated the sentiment of the era: "Marriage brings a man only two happy days. The day he takes his bride to bed and the day he lays her in her grave." The Romans didn't believe in the concept much either. Their excesses of the flesh legendary, Romans believed that marriage for love would get in the way of pleasure and duty. When Christianity ruled supreme, marriage and sex were for procreation only. Love never entered into it. Only through literature has the notion of marriage *for love* even been broached, and it wasn't until the late eighteenth century and early nineteenth century that humans even began thinking along those lines. In fact, *thinking* about finding true love was all most of us did until very recently. So, don't be so hard on yourself. Taking love into our own hands is still so new that we are just now in the process of getting it right.

And indeed, the divorce rate is skyrocketing but lest we forget, it is only since the mid 1950s, essentially after World War II, that divorce even became remotely acceptable. I remember when my grandmother came on Saturdays with news for my mother of the old neighborhood. When she told of the woman on the second floor whose husband had just filed for divorce, she lowered her voice! There was shame, and a feeling somehow of immorality attached to divorce. The statisticians would have us think that marriages of yesteryear were somehow happier unions. They weren't necessarily happier, even if the bonds were indeed tighter. Divorce was simply an unacceptable exit. Couples stayed together for the children and also because of blatant economics. A woman had precious few choices then. She was a *homemaker* in the majority of cases. In an unhappy marriage, a man, and to a much lesser extent a woman, either had an affair or they simply endured.

The couple who lived next door to my parents while I was growing up were a perfect example. He drank and played around, and she went to Bingo. They weren't ever candidates for divorce, being strict Catholics. Everyone ate and drank as they celebrated their fortieth wedding anniversary, but was it a happy union? I think not.

Even the *grounds* for divorce have shifted. Years ago, abuse and adultery were barely tolerated as the only acceptable outs; today, irreconcilable differences will suffice. Until about 1935, there wasn't even anything remotely like marital therapy. Clergymen counseled troubled couples into bearing the brunt. So the argument that the divorce rate is higher today than it was thirty years ago because we're doing something *wrong*, doesn't hold water. It's like comparing apples and cherries. They're both red and have stems but that's where the similarities end.

Personally, I don't particularly care to argue either way; it's like deciding which came first, the chicken or the egg? Some people remember the "good ol' days" as good, just because they're old. I'd prefer to start from ground zero and build a better mousetrap. Now that I'm armed with information about who I am, the choices that are open to me, what I want and what direction I want to move towards, I am better equipped to find the person I want to move in that direction with. We've all seen firsthand which relationships we want to emulate and those we don't. In the 1990s we have the opportunity to take all this knowledge and process it to create the kind of union that will work and bring us joy, and that will hopefully set the new standard for the turn of the century.

The best thing this book can give you at this very moment is the chance to take a deep breath. It can offer the realization that old habits and ideas die hard and it can offer the understanding of how men really think and how they really feel, *deep-down*. By doing so, this book will help you understand and forgive the trespasses that have led some to behave as they do, as it helps you to choose the path that hopefully, leads to finding the partner that will provide you with long-term, nurturing and lasting love. In the process, it will give you the license and tools you need to enjoy your life as a single person, *right now*!

Chapter 3

Living Happily Ever After ... Even *Before* Marriage

Being single need not be looked upon as simply getting from point "A" to point "B." Worse, some among us view the time between parents to marriage or from marriage to marriage as a perilous mine field, begat with sadistic pygmies blowing poison darts at every turn. "Whoa," *I dodged another one.* "Yikes," *that was a close call.* "Please God, just let me survive until the right one comes along."

This doesn't have to be the case. Bob from Indianapolis is a great example. Tall, blonde and muscular, he does not look at all near his forty-five years of age. "I was married right out of college to my high school sweetheart. We had two kids, moved into three different houses, each one bigger than the last, and somehow grew apart. I went through days, no actually years," he said getting visibly emotional, "feeling so empty and lonely... and guilty for feeling like that. I tried so hard to make her happy. She wanted the kids to be raised Methodist, so I converted; she wanted us to join a local country club, so we did. We took tennis lessons; we traveled to Mexico, Hawaii and went on, what were supposed to be, romantic cruises. Nothing seemed to bring us together, and each time something didn't work, she got more miserable, as I tried harder and harder to figure out what was wrong, and why I never seemed able to make her happy. I never went out with the boys, never drank, but I always felt like I was just going through the motions. I was afraid to talk to anyone because it's always women who complain about this kind of stuff, not men. I concentrated on my job, on my kids and just trying to keep that empty feeling from coming to the surface.

"Then one day, she woke up like every other day, except she announced before I had even brushed my teeth that she was tired of living with someone incapable of making her happy and was going to file for divorce. That was it. No, 'Let's talk,' or 'Let's see someone for counseling,' no nothin' like you see in the movies. I left for work that day in a fog that didn't lift, until one Saturday, when my girls and I were having McMuffins and juice at McDonald's about nine months after the divorce, and I asked them what they wanted to do now? They asked, 'Daddy, can we go to the beach?' It occurred to me in that split second, that my wife would have said, 'In a couple of hours, after your meal settles.' I was able to say, 'okay,' and we took off for the lake. Right then it occurred to me; I could finally do some of the things that I wanted to do, *when* I wanted to do them! I've spent the last three years since my divorce getting in touch with the child inside me that had been squelched for so long. Now that I found him, I'm never going to let anyone take him away from me again.

"I always wanted to take up golf; she always thought it was boring and too expensive. I'm now the proud owner of a set of Jack Nicklaus clubs and a pretty decent handicap. I've spent these years getting in touch with Bob. I forgot what I liked to do and what I liked to eat. I never read a book my whole married life, isn't that ridiculous? I somehow felt guilty that I wasn't doing something to improve the house. I've spent three years catching up."

And what about women? "There have been a few," he said. "I just didn't think it fair to get into a relationship again until I was sure who Bob was. Now I am. I've experienced women who understand the concept of sharing and of making each other happy. Sharing interests and likes. Being single these few years has been such a freedom, such a wonderful time for me to explore and *like* Bob. For me to draw the boundaries that cannot be crossed again in allowing me to stay healthy and whole. But I *do* miss being a couple. I miss having that one special someone. I don't enjoy the single bars, or the game-playing. I never did. To me, that's work and I already have a job, that's why I came to *the BACHELOR BOOK*."

Bob's post-divorce experience is a glorious example of someone using his solo years to bring about introspection, pleasure and freedom. Women are usually accused of "allowing" what happened to Bob, to happen to them. Of becoming chameleons to please their partners, and losing sight of themselves. We don't realize how many men are plagued by the same feelings—the fear and resentment of having to be all things to one person. By far, the vast majority of men sing the praises of a woman who "has her own life and her own interests." This is powerfully attractive to men and I can't stress its impact enough.

This is the first and perhaps most important step to moving Alice from her home in Purgatory to a grand new residence right smack in the middle of Wonderland.

"I want a woman I can learn from," said a thirty-eight year-old anesthetist. "Someone who does not have to rely on me to make her happy. I want someone who already gets pleasure from her life. My first really long-term meaningful relationship was while I did my residency. During that time you're working like an animal just to get to the next level. I just remember what a burden it was to me, having always to think up and provide the outlets in our relationship. She had friends but always wanted to see the movie with me, eat at a new restaurant with me first, go to an opening or concert just with me. In the beginning it was flattering, that a woman you love appreciates your company enough that she wants to experience things with you as shared time. But when my job and schedule were such that I just couldn't manage the time off, and she really wanted to go, she'd get all quiet and pissed off and refused to go. No amount of reassuring her that I didn't mind, or that I was pleased she'd have the opportunity to go with a friend if I couldn't, would budge her. It got to the point that the pressure of having to *participate* to ensure her happiness, got too great to bear. Two years ago, I met a travel writer who loves flea markets, off-the-wall animated movies, and of all things, hot air ballooning. I was scared sh..tless, the first time she made me go up, but did you ever try making love while hovering over the treetops? Every day with this gal is an adventure. And if I don't want to go, or can't go somewhere, she *will* go and have a good time anyway and then tell me all about it when we finally get home together. I love and have great respect for her independence and I appreciate how much that independence takes the pressure off me."

"I love and have great admiration for a woman who wants me, desires me and likes me... but who doesn't *need* me to affirm her worth," said a forty-four year old divorced father of two teens. "That way if a situation I can't control comes up, she isn't dependent on me. There are a lot of women out there who pit themselves against my children. I'm a responsible man and I make time for the woman in my life, but I also take my responsibilities as a father seriously. A woman with little self-esteem views those times I choose to spend with my kids, instead of her, as an aspersion. That kind of woman is too much responsibility for me."

We need to redefine what it means to be single, to update the guidelines and to educate people about the benefits and vitality of this time prioe to marriage. The closest thing we have to single-orientation is college. Yet college is still somewhat regimented and structured. Statistics prove that many marry just after graduation, before they have had any time to test their new-found freedom and maturity, losing so much of self-exploration time during that transition. Maybe if we all used the time prior to marriage, or for some of us, the interval between marriages, as a time to assess who we are, what's important to us, and what kind of life would really make us happy, and then set a course to realistically achieve it, there would be less divorce and discontent fifteen years down the road when we discover we took the wrong route.

If you're reading this book because you're involved in a relationship that's causing you pain, leaving you empty, or wracking you with doubt daily, you have to decide if it's worth repairing, and if it is, work at it as intelligently and diligently as if you were starting over again at the beginning. If you know deep down that the relationship you're in will never be better, if you're certain there's nothing that can be done to make it happier or healthier, you have a heart-wrenching decision to make. It is best that you put the car in reverse; back up, turn around, and learn all you can about the mistakes that were made, the potholes you and your partner fell into, and the hurts that could have been avoided before you start over again. And lastly, if you're reading this book because you're single now, you should feel wonderful and grateful. This time can be an incredible opportunity. Indulge yourself while you have the time to devote to you and only you. Pour some great bubbles in your bath and take a few extra moments to soak, look through the *what's happening* section of today's paper and find something you always wanted to do, but either haven't found the time to do it or the person to do it with and just throw caution to the wind, and make the necessary reservations. Take a class, join a club, volunteer at a needy organization or for a political candidate, spring for a series of massages or facials, learn to do a craft at your local art store, call your city government and ask if they are in need of help on any committees. I could fill this whole book with ideas. Just make a commitment to do one thing that you've said you wanted to do but haven't done. I know this sounds horribly contradictory, but doing this will bring you closer to establishing the fulfilling, healthy relationship you seek. Doing something different provides additional stimulation that many of us need to yank us out of a rut, even if we don't think we're in one. Not to mention that it puts you in different social situations as well.

Noreen's mother literally begged Noreen to join the class she was taking at a local junior college. All Noreen was doing was working, going to singles dances and the occasional bar. Like on the *Hunt for Red October*, Noreen was looking for a man. "You've got to do something different," her mother said. "You're not meeting anyone you're interested in anyway. At least do something you might enjoy. Remember when you used to love making things?"

"I don't have time to do something I enjoy," she barked at her mother. "I work a full-time job, and I take care of an apartment and two cats. I'll never get married if I just go with you and take-up basketweaving," came the typically callused answer. "I'm sure not going to be interested in a guy who'd be there on a Thursday night weaving baskets," Noreen told her mother.

That may be true. But boy, was she interested in the hunk who showed up after class to meet his basketweaving sister for a drink. The moral of the story? *Never say never.* Doing something good for yourself can give you the extra boost you need, and it can work out in more ways than one.

Chapter 4 | Understanding What Is Happening To Men In The '90s

While women are born feminine, societies insist that men *earn* their masculinity. And society has not been very generous if they didn't. Women can take solace in the fact that they're not alone in feeling insecure, vulnerable and bewildered. Men endure these emotions too, only they've been schooled at internalizing these feelings and trying to weather them alone. Women band together, pass around nine pints of low-fat ice milk and compare notes.

"I remember feeling very alone growing up," said Barry, a forty-three year old commerical artist. "My mother and sister always seemed to have this invisible bond and my sister could cry and be comforted by my mother. She seemed to be able to tell mom anything. I couldn't do that with dad. I couldn't cry if I got hurt or sad. He seemed to always expect me to tough it out. I remember being envious of my sister, not for any other reason than she was able to express how she felt—and was comforted by it."

With women striving to find identity and balance in their own lives, relationships have suffered. There wasn't a dry eye in the audience of a national Canadian TV show when fifty-one year old Derek, a Toronto businessman said, "For twenty-eight years, I was just a husband and father. That's all I knew. That's what I was happy doing. When my wife asked for a divorce to 'find herself,' I walked around in a daze. I'm lonely and I miss my life. I don't even know how to be single. I wasn't very adept at it the first time either."

Men are not the enemy here. They are as confused and unsure as we are. We now have a generation of people who are trying to find professional direction and personal equilibrium. Many of the recent changes, most notably the Women's Movement, have impacted the dynamics of today's relationships. "I brought a flower home to my wife almost every day of our seventeen years together. I said, 'I love you!' every morning, and made sure to say it every night. I thought our sex life was great. She goes out and has an affair because she felt *unfulfilled*, and then says she wants a divorce," said a forty-five year-old Minneapolis airline pilot. "Can you tell me what I did wrong?"

Many of the men I've interviewed over the years talk openly about their vulnerability and their own self-esteem with respect to changing times, changing roles and changing expectations. For all the wondrous latitudes and freedoms won for us by the Women's Movement, relationships lay in the wake as the casualties. And it's not because anyone did anything wrong. There is no one and nothing on which to lay blame, as many opt to do when a situation has gone awry. The only thing that has happened here is that time and progress upset the apple cart. It's like sitting down to play a game of Monopoly and someone suddenly changes some of the rules. You're still basically able to play, you're just not quite sure how to go about it.

"That's kind of how I feel," said Stan, a fifty-six year-old printer. "I was raised to be strong, keep my emotions to myself and to be a man. Don't cry, don't complain, don't let my guard down. After the divorce, I'm meeting women who constantly want to know how *I feel*. Well, I'm not exactly sure how I feel. I'm even less sure of how to express it. I always felt I was asked to pay too high a price for *being a man*. Now, that I have the opportunity to show my emotions, I'm afraid to. I'm afraid I'll be labeled less than a man. I'm afraid I'll be looked at as weak. I didn't like the way things were, but I'm even more terrified of how they are now."

Thousands of years ago when we went from the singular caveman mentality to that of the one leader tribal mentality, the transition didn't go very smoothly either. Each of the tribe's powerful men challenged the leader time and time again until a flow that was livable was settled upon. And the transition from arranged marriages to those of free choice followed much the same course. When the son of a prominent Jewish family eloped with an Italian girl from the neighborhood, rather than marry the daughter of a Jewish diamond merchant in just the 1950s, the Jewish mother wore black, threatened to put her head in the oven and the family mourned the son as dead, literally casting him off from the family. What a colossal waste in a life that's so short. But that's what happened even just twenty-five years ago when you married outside your religion.

Traditions and expectations die hard, very hard. Transition is not something we adapt to easily. The rules may not make us happy, but swimming against the current isn't a sure thing either. Think for a minute: the only difference the monumental transitions of yesteryear made toward modernization, and the power, equality shift brought about by the Women's Movement, is that *WE are living in the midst of these changes*. A hundred years from now, the problems, concerns and challenges we're experiencing trying to carve out new perimeters for a happy life, much the same as Lewis and Clark carved out new frontiers in America, will be documented in history books for our great granddaughters to read. We're making history, and in doing so, we're bound to make mistakes before we get it right.

We spend too much precious time in the '90s trying to point fingers and figure out who's at fault. Some men claim the reason they can't form lasting bonds is because the Women's Movement produced bossy, pushy women who only want to get even for the inequality of the last 200 years. Women claim the discontent stems from men's unwillingness to relinquish their supreme, previously unchallenged control. Again, what came first, the chicken or the egg? Do you really care? Or do you really just want to concentrate on learning to co-exist happily, and build a fulfilling life in the here and now?

I'm so grateful to the Betty Friedans and Gloria Steinems who paved the way for me to achieve my potential or at least have provided me with the opportunity. I'm indebted to them for giving me the choice to be a mommy or not, and the opportunity to do both should I care to (and have the stamina). If there's any finger pointing going on, you won't see my short, stumpy digit in the pack. When the opportunity to leave the kitchen and enter the workplace was first presented to us, we sprinted in droves, taking our rightful places in almost every field. Now, some thirty odd years later, many of us who chanted, "I am woman, hear me roar," replace it with, "I am woman, hear me yawn." We're dead tired of bringing home the bacon, frying it up in the pan and never, ever letting him forget he's a man. We don't even know who we are half the time. Having and doing it all is exhausting. But the Women's Movement gave us the choice and changed the dynamics of relationships forever. If *we're* confused about the course our lives should take, *men* are completely stymied.

"Janna and I went together since our junior year of college. In our second year of law school she said she wanted to have a baby and start a family. I tried to convince her to finish school and take the bar, but she said she was tired of school, tired of the pressures to achieve and knew that she wanted to be a mommy and that raising a healthy, stable family was just as important and gratifying to her. And that's what we did. Three kids later, I was made partner in my firm, we had a summer cottage and a $600,000 home in upstate New York. One morning over orange juice, she tells me she's feeling unappreciated and unproductive and tells me it's my fault; that while she was keeping the home hearth burning, I was off establishing a great life and career for myself. She files for divorce. I still don't know what hit me. In the settlement, I'm paying for her to finish her *interrupted law degree."*

Men are as plagued by not knowing what to do, what to say, how to react or *if* they should react at all and when. Men who suggest they themselves are consistently being hurt by women—of being caught between the contradiction of what women say they want, and what they ultimately choose. We are to be held equally accountable for the present difficulty in finding fulfillment today and if we are to bridge the gap, we must be charitable and forgiving, understanding that men—most normal, caring, and loving men, are also doing the best they can with the new rules provided them. In a world where for hundreds of years women were told to zig and suddenly, along comes the Women's Movement saying, "Hey, ladies, over here... it's now perfectly acceptable to zag," I think we've changed course pretty well. Sure we've crashed into a few walls, and those collisions hurt and sometimes make us fearful of other crashes. But, as women, we persevere, sometimes hitting that wall several times over. But as we walk away, rubbing our bruised egos and plotting our next run at the wall, pity the poor man that either had to jump out of our way or who crashed into the wall right alongside us.

Consider that the men of today are, for the most part, decent human beings who also seek love, companionship and BALANCE. Don't judge them too harshly for zigging when you'd prefer they zagged. Remember that we're in this together. Men are as confused as we are. They too feel the burden to fulfill and then merge their traditional role with their new roles. Men are also caught between dual expectations just like we are. "I'm supposed to be the Wall Street wizard by day, wheeling and dealing and cutting the throat of anyone who stands still long enough," says Lawrence, a forty-six year old stock-broker. "Then I'm supposed to come home at night and be the vulnerable, sensitive Kevin Costner clone. I try. I sincerely try, but I can't do it... at least not all the time.

Change is slow. We must have empathy and tolerance for

men. Their frustrations are not unlike our own. It's far more productive to learn to understand men, than to stay at odds with them.

Chapter 5 | Successfully Single—Embarking On The Journey

When I speak to singles I always ask them to treat their single years as a journey, *preparing* them for marriage. Inevitably, there are smirks and self-conscious giggles at the proposed silliness of the drill until I equate it with a journey deep within the jungles of the Amazon. Would you like to be dropped on your head from a plane with nothing more than food and extra clothes? I think not. Even though those provisions are survival staples, perhaps a map to get you the hell out of there would be nice too. And hey, a good navigational map showing you how to avoid life-threatening dangers and pointing out the awe inspiring waterfalls and scenic beauty along the way might even allow you to *enjoy* the trip. That's what having discovered your expectations during your single years can do for you after you have decided to marry. There is nothing more gratifying than building an everlasting love and a life with a person who's really your soulmate. And, it's not hard to do. It's just time consuming, and like everything else in life that's worth achieving, it takes the dirtiest of all four letter words—work. I hate to belabor the point again, but it's just like a diet. You can drink that liquid stuff until you shrink down to Olive Oyl, but unless you alter your lifestyle and learn the correct way to eat, exercise and manage your weight, you'll eventually balloon back up. Or in the case of relationships, be back out buying the next great singles book eight years from now.

An interesting point to note here is that the incidence of remarriage to a previous partner is also escalating. How can that be possible? If we were dissatisfied enough to divorce them how can we tolerate another union with them? Tom, a forty year old patent attorney who applied to *the Bachelor Book,* is a case in point. "After being divorced from Trina for almost three years, I started to reevaluate the things that I felt tore us apart, he explained. "I also dated quite a bit and never really found anyone I enjoyed being with more."

As I interviewed Tom, it became abundantly apparent to me that this man still had strong feelings for his ex-wife, and an unresolved yearning for what might have been. "We were just fighting so much that last year of our marriage, that it overshadowed everything. We withheld sex from each other to punish each other; we hardly spoke, and when we did it was sharply and with agitation. We both started to grate on each other. Habits like her chronic lateness were cute in the beginning, but got progressively more irritating. If I brought up something about her that bothered me, she brought up two of mine that bothered her. But in our years apart, I realized that we let all those tiny things pile up instead of resolving them one by one and learning to compromise."

"It sounds as though you've thought about this a lot," I said. "Have you ever thought of telling her?"

"As a matter of fact I have," he admitted. "I've just never done it."

"What's the worst that could happen?" I suggested. "If she doesn't feel the same, at least you can put it behind you and move on. The way you feel now, you're sort of stuck in limbo."

He never made it into the magazine. He and Trina remarried a year and a half later, announced the postcard I got from Costa Rica. After two years of seeing who else was out there, and having time away from the problems to assess them fairly, they each decided that the devil they knew was better than the devil they didn't. They each used the time apart, *their single years*, as a learning opportunity and discovered that it wasn't that they didn't love each other, it was just that they were both miserable with the life they were living together. I hope that they took the time to redefine old boundaries and establish new ones for the second time around.

At the TV show "AM Philadelphia" one very rainy morning, a beautiful woman with long dark hair and a great smile stood up, and as the cameras were rolling, said, "I've been a blonde, a redhead and a brunette. I've had blue contacts, green ones and even Liz Taylor violet. I've done it all; why can't I find a man?" The part of my answer that got on camera was that "It isn't the color of your hair or eyes." I told her she could have Kermit-colored hair, she'd still be beautiful. It's four things: 1) knowing who she is, 2) understanding what she's projecting about that to other people, 3) knowing what kind of relationship and partner she's most compatible with and 4) sheer opportunity.

Off camera, I told her what my grandmother in her infinite wisdom always told me: "Mindela, if what you're doing isn't working out the way you want it to, the best thing to do is go back and start at the beginning."

Her simple and uncomplicated advice reverberates time and time again in my ears, whenever I'm completely perplexed by whatever task I undertake. In every instance, the extra moments spent in reflection seem to solve the problem. This can be especially symbolic for singles looking to find enduring love.

I hope these first five chapters have made you feel better, and have shown you that the situation you're in is not unalterable, and that you certainly are not in it alone. Hopefully, you've taken the time to think about who you are, what's important to you and where you want to go. But don't be so concerned with arrival that you neglect to enjoy the trip.

In the next part of the book you'll learn how to expand your man-meeting opportunities, improve your chances of meeting those that are truly suitable and how to determine the difference. You'll discover how to unlock your own desirability and discover the truth about what does and does not appeal to most men. If you will make the commitment and allow it, this book will assist you in finding the partner who is right for you or at the very least, it will bring you closer than you've ever come before.

Part Three
How To Meet A man

Chapter 6

Man Finding—Let Me Count The Ways

Ding Dong! the doorbell screams. "Just a minute," you call out in your sexiest Joan Crawford voice as you put your negligee's matching marabou and glass slippers on your newly pedicured feet. When you open the door it's Prince Ever-so-Charming, with chocolates, flowers and a rock the size of one of Liz Taylor's violet eyeballs. "Will you marry me?" he asks on bended knee. Your mind races all a flutter, "Gee, I hope he remembered to park his white horse in the visitor's parking spot."

Wake u-up! You're either dreaming or you mixed your Nyquil with too many antihistamines again. That's the stuff romance novels are made of. The reality of the situation is that before the proposal must come an initial meeting, then the first date, then hopefully, the second. But what's a girl to do? If you can't bear another Saturday night of Lean Cuisine and your VCR, read on.

In this segment we'll first explore some of the alternative avenues that women have for meeting men. Some you are more than aware of, some you may be remotely familiar with, and some may be as foreign to you as Pig Latin. Don't immediately write off any of them until you really consider them. Next, we'll discuss the things that you can do to make yourself irresistible to men. Again, Rome wasn't built in a day. If I had a magic potion for turning "vivacious and cute" into a combo of Carol Alt and Cher, I would have guzzled it all myself (and left none for you. Hey, I'm a team player but I'm not stupid).

This book cannot guarantee any quick fixes but it can arm you with information, giving you a distinct edge and discernible confidence. I have interviewed thousands of men and I'm sharing the valuable exchange with you. I've sorted through and compiled what men of all ages, walks of life, lifestyle and income brackets; want, admire, cherish, respect, regard, savor and appreciate, and the things they absolutely don't. From the first date through several, this segment will lead you closer to finding a man, determining if he's right for you, and if he is, in the next segment you'll learn how to turn that relationship into a lifetime partnership.

How do you get started? How do you take the first step?

"Wait," I hear some of you saying. "I have to get a complete make-over, trade my lifetime supply of nachos and Ben and Jerry's Heath Bar Crunch for sprouts and tofu and I have to move. I don't want Prince Charming coming to this dump."

Not!

RULES OF THUMB TO ALWAYS REMEMBER

RULE NUMBER 1: NOTHING VENTURED, NOTHING GAINED.

I'd love to quote Plato or Aristotle or someone more eloquent here, but Publisher's Clearing House says it best: "If you don't enter, you can't win."

"Please come out tonight," Beth pleaded with her best friend Sue at 11 am. "I've been eying this guy every Friday for weeks at Bimini Boat Club and Monday I bumped into him at the bank and he said, 'Maybe I'll see you on Friday.' I've got to be there tonight and I can't go alone."

"I'm just getting over a cold," Sue complained. "My nose is raw and redder than Rudolph's; my hair is a wreck and all I'm going to do tonight is watch *Picket Fences* and take a bath."

At 4:30 in the afternoon Sue's phone rang again. "I've called everyone I know," Beth continued her plea. "Even some women I don't like, and no one is available tonight. You're my best friend and if you love me you'll come with me. You know I'd do it for you."

"Have you been getting pointers from my mother?" Sue thought as guilt overtook her better judgment. "All right, all right, I'll go, but I won't have a good time and then you'll owe me—Big."

At about midnight, as Beth was gazing deeply into Mr. Bimini's eyes, Sue was on her eleventh tissue. As she was recovering from her latest sneezing jag, a landscape architect with a great voice said, "I had a killer cold like that last month. I thought I was going to die."

Sue thought for sure she must have died while she was sneezing. Where else but Heaven would a guy who could obviously choose many other women, especially one who wasn't breathing through her mouth, talk to a red nosed, one eyed, germ-spreading, tissue-bearer? As he offered to buy her an orange juice, they chatted about colds.

So many women put off doing *anything* until *everything* seems perfect, thus becoming prisoners of inertia. There is a distinct emotional advantage when you look and feel good, but you don't have to wait until you lose fifteen pounds, grow your bad haircut back out, work off your thighs or move to a better neighborhood... if you wait for all your ducks to line up, you'll likely be in a rocking chair with your dancing shoes still in their original box thirty years later. But, having said that, the more attractive you feel, the more confidence you project. And I've dedicated a whole chapter to seduction and desirability (See Chapter 9). Having a manicure so you're not running around with chipped, uneven nails,(which probably wouldn't keep a potential Mr. Right from approaching you) certainly might keep *you* from rebuffing him because *you* don't feel quite right.

I was in high school when "maxi" coats were all the rage. Remember those long coats that came to your ankle? When I first got mine, I was so proud and so sure I looked cool. My friends and I (all in maxi's) had just walked a few short blocks between school and the local supermarket through slush and ice. It was so cold and I was walking so fast that when the automatic doors opened, I sped in. It was the split second that I stepped off the rubber entrance mat and onto the highly polished linoleum that the ice on the heels of my boots caused me to go down like a ton of bricks. That wasn't the bad part. The maxi coat acted like a magic carpet and I careened, spread-eagle, down the produce aisle right into a huge display of Chiquita bananas which came crashing down on top of me. All I heard, since I couldn't see (I was covered in bananas), was the sound of convulsive laughter all around me. The guy who ultimately helped me up, ended up asking me out. Talk about inopportune moments!

Rule number 2: You are fine the way you are.

As women, we get caught up in thinking we have to be perfect or we shouldn't bother at all. My grandmother always told me "There's a cover for every pot." That's true when you're seeking unconditional love rather than merely conditional approval. Look around and watch couples. On a recent trip to Atlantic City, while I was having breakfast at one of the restaurants with a huge window on the boardwalk, I saw couples in every size and shape go by. Most people looked a lot like their partners. We feel best when the people we love and the people who love us, mirror us to some extent. It makes us feel safe and accepted. Sure, opposites may attract but commonality is what will keep you together. Tall, athletic men were, for the most part, with tall athletic women. Short dark women seemed to choose short dark men. Trendy went with trendy, clean and pressed were with clean and pressed and rumpled and mismatched seemed to be happy with other rumpled and mismatched. The couple who caught my eye were on a bench directly across from my window. She sat down with a *USA Today* and he with *The Wall Street Journal*. They each read their respective papers and when they finished, they got up, ditched the papers in the trash and took off. I think Noah and my grandmother are right.

"I've written and talked on the phone with at least five of your bachelors and had a wonderful rapport with each of them," wrote a 280 pound hairdresser from Vancouver, British Columbia. "But I don't think your BACHELOR BOOK magazine really works, or it hasn't for me. As soon as I send them my picture I never hear from them again. I don't think I will renew my subscription." In researching whom she had written to, each had clearly stated they were looking for an active, slim, athletic woman. Our magazines are a lot of things, but wish books they're not. We can't create chemistry where there is none. Many times we hope the object of our affection will be so attracted to the wonderful person we are on the inside, they'll forgo their physical preferences or age requirements. For the one time that happens, there are probably 10,000 when it doesn't. You can lead a horse to water, but you cannot make him drink, especially if water is not his preference.

Not only will you feel more secure and comfortable with someone who's compatible, you'll feel as though you've come home and found your favorite pair of fuzzy slippers. Finding someone who accepts you unconditionally, just as you are, is your absolute best opportunity for targeting long-term happiness. We've all either had or seen relationships between two "friends" so compatible, they provide comfort and support for each other in almost every situation, yet one thinks of the other only as a friend claiming no physical attraction. People buy into the love-at-first-sight myth we're bombarded with in movies, romance novels and soap operas, believing that if the "attraction" isn't instantaneous, like Cupid's arrow hitting us between the eyes, it isn't as meaningful. But, true love can also be *cultivated*.

"When I first met Emilio," says Ellen Moore, head of Mensa's special interest group *Singles Network*, "I don't think either of us had 'instant chemistry', but we had been speaking on the phone almost three months before we met and had established such an emotional, intellectual and spiritual rapport that we knew we had to meet. When we did, there wasn't this tear-your-clothes-off chemistry, but there was something special enough to know we wanted to be together. I moved from Missouri to New York, where Emilio was living, and one year later we married. We didn't just have 'sizzle' and then try to match everything up; we did it the other way around."

This does happen in some cases, but don't get delusional; it won't work in every case. Just because you want someone and do almost everything right, you can't force him to want you. But I also wish I had a nickel for every time I heard a man say "When I was twenty-five, there once was this girl I let get away; I just didn't recognize what I felt for her as love," or the woman who says, "I never was interested in him because I thought he was too nice, we were too similar; it wasn't enough of a challenge. Had I only realized." Hindsight is always 20/20 and I want to strangle people who have gone through fifteen years of "challenging" relationships and still wouldn't know the right person if he or she sat in their lap.

RULE NUMBER 3: BE HONEST.

If you're going to make the effort to find a man who has the potential to be Mr. Right instead of just Mr. Right Now, you need to present a clear and accurate picture of who you are.

"If you write in my bio that I'm looking for a traditional woman who is more interested in being a wife than a career woman, I won't get as many responses," said a twenty-nine year-old importer from Portland, Oregon. "The whole idea," we explained to him, "is not to stuff your mailbox full with 400 maybes—*that's* feeding your ego. It's to be specific enough to put fifty or sixty *very* possibles in there. Hopefully, if you're lucky, out of those, you'll narrow it down to someone who blows your socks off and is right for you... for the long run."

Don't let your ego get in the way. If you're much more cerebral than physical, don't try to give the impression you're a swashbuckling, female merchant marine. Before you make the effort to find who's right for you, make sure you have a clear picture of who you are and what you have to offer (See the self-discovery test in Chapter 15). Singles need to stop trying to pound square pegs into round holes. Why go through hurt and unnecessary rejection, when a little detective work can help bring you closer to the cover for *your* pot, whatever size it might be? And the good news is, some of the work has been done for you. On the following pages you'll find a run-down of many of the alternative avenues open to singles, followed by a resource directory of special interest groups. There is a wealth of clubs, organizations, magazines and newsletters specifically for those who fit more snugly into a certain category. Groups comprised of heavy women and the men who love them, tall people, single parents, Mensa candidates, people who share certain interests and many, many others.

The key to finding a partner who'll be attracted to you is knowing where to look.

DATING ALTERNATIVES
THE PERSONALS

In the Gold Rush days, it was a legitimate way for miners out west to meet women, and hence, the mail-order bride concept was born. In the late 1960's, almost a hundred years later, when the first few "personal ads" appeared in alternative publications like New York's *Village Voice*, most people thought they were kinky and got a kick out of reading the outlandish requests. "French maid's uniform required for afternoon cleaning. Feather duster provided" or "Italian Stallion needs to be saddle-broken. Only those with spurs and riding crops need apply." The people who placed these ads were wacked out and bizarre, down and desperate, right? Surely, no nice person would consider placing one.

That was then and this is now. Almost thirty years and a major attitude adjustment later, every major newspaper and magazine in this country, and now several other countries, have huge sections filled with an abundance of ads with itty bitty print and strange symbols that seem to be written by aliens on mind altering substances. SWCDF N/S, N/D, seeks S/W or B/CDM who's financially, emotionally stable. Prof., pref., 30-40 ??????

The first time I read the *Personals* I thought they were some weird eye tests and those who could decipher them could toss away their glasses and contacts and shout, "It's a miracle! I've been cured, praise the Classified editor!"

Most major papers don't want to admit the impressive effect that personals advertising is having on their bottom lines, and many of the people who use them still don't want to admit they do.

The upside – They're quick. Most ads will run within a week after you place them, some the next day. They're targeted. Most people only place and read ads from a small localized area so you can indeed find someone to date almost immediately. And they're relatively inexpensive ranging from free to approximately $40-$50, depending upon the number of words. Most now require a voice mail option which is either free or charges you the same amount of money to retrieve your messages as it does the person who left the message for you.

The downside – Decoding the Personals can be a real brain teaser. Carla, the lovable quick talking, quick-witted waitress on the old sitcom *Cheers* says there is one basic principle for advertising in the personals: "Lie!" The fact that the ads are blind means you never exactly know what you're getting. The Personals is where the phrase, "Beauty is in the eye of the beholder" really becomes meaningful. Buzz words like "young professional" could mean anything from a twenty-two year old teacher to a fifty year old hooker. "Huggable" can mean anything from carting around a few extra pounds to being able to crush the life out of you with a single hello. And they can be dangerous. You do not know who placed the ad or what agenda they had for doing so. It's an easy entree for marrieds with a wandering eye, or worse. Since they're not regulated or screened, you're left to your own devices. Under no circumstances should you ever give anyone your home phone or address and always meet them in a very public place until you get to know them well. A further caution: the phone companies' Caller ID feature allows the person you are phoning to display your number and there are plenty of service bureaus in this country that will match the number with an address for a simple fee. So use caution.

BARS

Everyone hates them, yet if you drive by at 11:45pm, they're packed. Someone has to be going there. "Bars and clubs are a place to go and have fun with your friends," offered twenty-five year-old Joshua. "It's not a place to go with the intention of meeting the man or woman of your dreams. I have a good time when I go, it's like an instant party. But it also can be pretty lonely... and pretty sad. There are a lot of people who go, just because they have nowhere else to."

Bars are a place to get dressed up, down, wear western attire or stuff you'd only be caught dead in on Halloween. It's heady and exciting (also boring, especially if you don't drink) at times because there is always the possibility "the right one" will be there.

The upside – They're filled with people and they can be as cheap or expensive as you allow them to be. Some have a cover, (the fee just to enter) and others just charge you for what you drink. It's a place to go for the opportunity to meet someone; most times you don't have to travel far, and if you *do* meet someone, most likely they're from your local area.

The downside – Chances are Mr. Perfect could indeed be there... only three feet down the bar in fact, but with the noise level, the crowds, and all the frenetic energy, you might need one of those metal detectors people at the beach use to find buried coins in order to sniff him out. Bars are not conducive to stimulating conversation. "Y-E-E-S, I L-I-K-E M-OO-V-I-E-S TOO."

"What??"

(louder) "I L-I-K-E M-OO-V-I-E-S, T-O-OO!!

"WHAT??" - You get the idea.

The other caution is that you could spend the whole evening speaking to Mr. Damn-near-close-to-perfect only to find out that Mrs. Damn-near-close-to-perfect is at home waiting for him. It's like the old show, *"Queen for a Day"*; in a bar, anyone can be single for a night. And when the lights come on, it can be a scary, scary place.

MATCHMAKERS

They range from the time-honored shtetls whose, "have I got a match for you," brought a blush to a young woman's face, to the slick, plush carpeted glass and mirrored offices of today's high-end yentas, matchmakers are a hands-on approach to finding a partner. Some matchmakers work with a large staff who screen prospectives, organize dates, and do everything from the interviews to arranging the dates. Other matchmakers work alone and know every client personally. The cost? Expensive. Matchmakers can run from several thousands to many thousands. Generally between $3,000 and $11,000.

The upside – Matchmakers usually have a smaller clientele, so they are able to know each applicant personally and therefore more intimately. They are able to convey those qualities to a prospective mate with the enthusiasm of a friend. It is easier for some people to convey their wants and needs to one person only and to know that person will act on their behalf. Additionally, a well respected, well known matchmaker can have a very exclusive clientele, so if you can afford the fee, you can be certain that you're probably in good company. Many busy single executives use matchmakers the same way they would a personnel service. It's easier and less time consuming to have a professional do the searching and screening.

The downside – The expense is considerable and you must ask the matchmaker to give you written documentation explaining exactly how many matches that money entitles you to. Some matchmakers have been in business successfully for years, and have impeccable reputations while others have been sued many times. Years ago there was a highly publicized case filed by New York's State Attorney General against matchmaker Helena Amram by almost fifty complainants accusing her of overcharging and fraud. Caveat emptor—"let the buyer beware," has never been so apropos. Ask for references. Ask to see documentation of successful matches they've arranged and do your homework—check the county courthouse records to see if the firm or person you are considering using has ever been sued. Once or twice can be misunderstandings; more than that could be a problem; ... and carefully read the contract and ask your questions before you sign.

Video Dating

A service provided by a franchise or independent company where you are given a questionnaire to fill out and then are video-taped, doing your best to look relaxed and natural with bright lights in your eyes and a bunch of people you don't know milling around while you struggle to appear intelligent and witty. Your profile and video are cataloged and you have the opportunity to come in at your leisure and sift through "member" books until you pick out someone who strikes your fancy. Other members have the same option. If you're the picker, you are led to a small room with a VCR and TV monitor where you can privately view the tape(s), of the men you selected. If you like what you see on the tape(s) the service generally calls or sends a postcard to the persons you're interested in, informing them they've been selected. They are asked to come in to view the tape of the person who picked them, and if they also like what they see, the service provides each with the other's phone number so they can talk person-to-person. If the "pickee" is not interested in the "picker", then nothing happens. These services abound in the phone books in every major metropolitan area, (somewhat fewer in less dense areas) so they're readily available. They're quick. You can be signed, sealed and in a video library along with the other members in a matter of a couple of weeks. They seldom turn anyone down, especially if you can afford the $500 - $3,000 cost.

The upside – Since they are somewhat expensive, most members know that the other member can at least afford the service. You are able to see what the person looks, sounds and acts like right away as opposed to a blind personal ad, so you can at least determine if there is any interest beyond the initial physicality. Your anonymity is protected. You are a number only in the video and the catalog. Most are open, extended hours so you can go when it's convenient. The people in the books are from your local area. You are able to choose your preferences: age, profession, height, coloring, etc. without offending anyone. And if someone is going to spend this kind of money, you can be relatively sure they are serious about wanting a relationship.

The downside – I may not be the most unbiased source of information about dating services. I have two file drawers filled with letters many penetrating letters from people who felt they were unfairly pressured into joining a dating service – and ultimately taken. "When I joined," said Ken, a thirty-one year old electrician, "I was told that there were tons of women in my age group available. But every time I picked one out of the book, they said those women weren't available. I started to think that maybe I was just not attractive to anyone, until I met a good-looking guy in the elevator. He said he was having the same problem. After a lot of groaning and complaining, my representative admitted that they were sorely short of young women but were working on remedying the problem and extended my membership. The only women who were picking me were women in their late thirties to late forties. I have nothing against older women, I just feel I was sold a bill of goods."

Jackie, a forty-five year old computer technician for the Social Security Administration, says much the same thing. "I wasn't sure I wanted to join but was given a FREE consultation card. Finally I decided I had nothing to lose and made the appointment. I'm certainly past the singles bar stage. I sat through the initial presentation, saw the film on the abundance of weddings and happy couples and was assigned to a representative who walked me through the place. I kept asking how much and she kept dodging the question. At the end, I was given various plans at prices that all exceeded $2,000. I was told if I joined right then I'd save 25%. She was very high pressure, reminding me how lonely I was. Assuring me it was the best decision I'd ever make. Well, I did join. I ended up spending $2500 and only getting three dates: a man who clearly had some emotional problems, an overweight comptroller who took me for Sushi and then home right after we ate, and a male-nurse who couldn't stop talking about his ex-wife and kids. There were lots of men in their thirties and early forties, but significantly fewer in my age group, most of whom said they wanted to start a family which indicated a preference for a younger woman. Of those I chose, I was told they were not available or already in relationships. When I inquired why their pictures were still in the books, they started to treat me as if I were simply a complainer. When I asked how it could be that no one I selected wanted to meet me, they sternly told me that perhaps I should work on making myself more attractive. During the sales pitch she told me how beautiful I was and that I'd be scooped up before the ink was dry. I just felt used and angry and when I asked for my money back they basically told me to get lost. Now I'm thinking of suing."

These stories weren't included to scare or dissuade you, simply to save you from making the wrong decision. As with everything, there are good dating services and bad ones. If the service exerts too much pressure on you to sign or will not allow you to think it over, or won't disclose the price until the end, walk away. Make sure the service you choose has been in business for a while and is reputable. Call the Better Business Bureau and the State Attorney General's office in your state and see if there are complaints on file. Ask the service representative if you can randomly call some other members in your age group, to get their opinion of the service. If they say no, ask if they have references you can call. Ask how often they update their files making sure they understand that you expect those files and therefore your choices to be current. Two or three of your choices being unavailable is a legitimate possibility, ten is unacceptable. Ask if all members are charged using the same scale. Several of our bachelors from around the country report dating services that offered them FREE memberships, or reduced price memberships because the dating service couldn't find enough men. Ask their ratio of men to women and what age groups they fall in. This is a service they are providing, and a service worth its price should not begrudge you this information. You wouldn't buy a car without driving it or doing some comparison shopping, why feel intimidated when it comes to your personal happiness? Try to put the payment on your credit card so that if you do have a legitimate complaint you have some recourse. It might sound like a lot of extra work to do, for something you hoped would free your time, but if you're going to spend $3,000, why take the chance of wasting it? You might as well go on a vacation or buy a new wardrobe; at least then you'll get something for your money.

In fairness to dating services, please understand that they can't perform miracles. If you're not attracting the Tom Cruise types in your real life, you can't expect a dating service to get him for you just because that's who you see yourself with. Also you can't be so rigid in your scrutiny of possible candidates, that no one fits the bill. If you're fifty-five and want someone thirty, yes, you need a service, just not this kind. Legitimate dating and introduction agencies perform a great service, but you as the consumer have every right to know exactly what you're buying PRIOR to purchasing. You can also contact ISIS - the International Society of Introduction Services at PO Box 31408, San Francisco, CA 94131 (415) 777-9769, founded in 1986, executive director Trish McDermott says that ISIS was formed to promote ethical advertising and business practices among introduction and dating services. "We have member organizations all over the country and we see that they adhere to a certain code of ethics. If they don't, we revoke their membership. We also will send anyone considering a dating service a list of questions they can ask when shopping for one so they can make a good decision," she said. "We'd be happy to send it to them if they call or write us," she added. Although they take no legal recourse against a shoddy company, they can log the complaint and lend a sympathetic ear.

COMPUTER OR INTERNET DATING

Welcome to the electronic highway and blind dating '90s style. With computers now readily available to just about anyone, they aren't being used just for business any more. Not by a long shot. You can shop, keep current, voice an opinion, make travel arrangements, write a letter to your sister and have it electronically sent to her before you could even get up and find a conventional envelope. Cyberspace is about to revolutionize socializing. All you need is a computer and a modem in order to access the various on-line services that tap into the Internet. (The vast global network that enables computers of all kinds to share services and communicate directly as if everyone were hooked into one giant computer. Internet reaches nearly twenty-five million computer users!!) Three of the largest are Prodigy (the largest), a cooperative effort between IBM and Sears (914-993-8000, telephone sign up 800-776-3449); America Online, one of the most popular (703-448-8700, telephone sign up 800-827-6364) and CompuServe, one of the original (614-457-0802, telephone sign up 800-848-8199). But there are dozens of others springing up almost daily. These companies provide a vast array of services, from paying your bills to booking a hotel. They offer almost unlimited business and technical resources and something called BBS (Bulletin Boards.) And there are thousands of these bulletin boards out there, covering practically any topic from Christianity to nude sunbathing. On-line users choose what is called a *Login ID*—a personal identification code that they use when calling their service. Now you're ready to send and receive E-mail (electronic mail)—messages that you type on your computer and send to others (and vice versa) on *your* electronic on-line service or others. That's one of the most time-efficient and interesting aspects, "letters" arrive almost instantly, even from abroad. Users pay a fee for getting on-line, either a flat rate or timed charges. Basic fees can be anywhere from about $8.95 a month to a lot more if you get hooked. Average timed fees are anywhere from ten to sixty dollars per hour.

The upside – There are over 60,000 computer bulletin boards in operation in the U.S., and more spring up daily. This means that while you peck away in Milwaukee, your message can be received by anyone who uses the service from coast to coast, including an enormous number of eligible men. And you can do it at your own pace. Can't sleep at 4am? Probably thousands of other people can't either. You can pick up and leave off as your schedule dictates, which makes it popular with single parents and those who work strange hours. People report several hundred responses from an "ad" on a bulletin board that if placed in a local paper, might yield only a scant few. There are also reports of intense meetings of the minds that can become deep and personal. You are getting to know someone on a profound level which can be stimulating and rich and difficult to achieve had you relied on looks only. And there are entire special interest groups that have created "rooms" where many people can be on-line at the same time, creating round-table discussions. These special interest groups (the over-forties, Big Beautiful Women and the men who love them, and many others) actually get to know and like each other so well that they arrange parties, weekends and holidays together. So if you feel out of place, or very singular, you can find a whole network on the computer, of people who either look or think like you.

The downside – The cost can get out of control for the hourly users as they peck away without watching the clock. You can also be pouring your heart out and falling in love with someone who may not be at all what they "peck" they are. There are thousands of people living vicarious lives through the characters they've created on the computer. There are also as many crazies using the computer as the personal ads, so under no circumstances reveal your true identity and check carefully with your provider to make sure they never reveal your actual identity to E-mail senders. The Internet, started originally by the government and used mainly by professors and universities, is not regulated and is as close to anarchy as you can get. They have their own rules and codes of conduct and it seems confounding until you get it right. Utilizing those providers that offer chat or talk options (Prodigy doesn't, so your messages are not instantaneous and may take minutes, hours or days to get a response—the other major on-line services do) is the same as talking on the phone, except you have to type everything you say. I don't know about you, but my mouth works faster than my fingers.

THE BACHELOR BOOK AND THE BACHELORETTE BOOK

Indulge me here. The reason I mention them, other than they're my personal favorites, is because they are a hybrid of many of the previous alternative avenues. Two separate "catalogs", they each feature 60-100 eligible men or women seeking relationships via a photograph, a 400-500 word biography and information where each may be individually contacted (by voice mail @ $1.95 per minute, or by letter—a two dollar fee covers same day forwarding) as well as other articles and features which are of interest to today's single. Both magazines are published every 3 1/2 to 4 1//2 months and are $31.25 for a five issue subscription.

The upside – You are able to see what each candidate looks like and read an unbiased in-depth profile written by a staff writer, which eliminates everyone calling themselves an attractive professional. The candidates have to pass a rigorous screening process and genuinely be seeking a long-term relationship in order to qualify for inclusion in the magazines. They are very inexpensive - one hundred dollar inclusion fee (or seventy-five dollars if you subscribe to one of the magazines) to be featured in either of the magazines, and your anonymity is protected since only your first name and the county and state you reside in are mentioned. Contact is limited to leaving messages on your voice mail or the company forwarding letters to you, so respondents cannot gain any access to you unless you decide they should have it. It's low-pressure, kind of like shopping by mail and you do so in the privacy of your own home. You know that respondents are already interested in you when you hear from them, and you can choose to respond to only those who interest you. Hundreds of weddings, live-together arrangements and friendships have been made as respondents are able to slowly get to know each other on a very personal and intimate level by being forced to become friends first, since geographically they may come from different areas.

The downside – Love interests may turn out to live 1200 miles away and many people may choose a bachelor or a bachelorette based on looks rather than mutual interests and reality and therefore may be disappointed if there's no communication. Since they are popular, there is generally a waiting list of about six months before you appear in an issue of the magazine. Complaints range from "Why can't you include two hundred men and women per issue instead of just eighty or so?" to "The magazines don't come out often enough; I hate to have to wait so long between them."

Chapter 7

The Resource Directory-
Clubs, Groups And Organizations To Help Your Ying Find Its Yang

I am the quintessential man-finder and this chapter is one of the preeminent gifts I can give you. It is a source you can use to help get you started ferreting out men. But not just any man, we're talking about Mr. Compatible instead of Mr. Square-Peg-that-I-now-have-to-fit-into-a-round-hole. The sources listed here are national; however, many have local chapters. Some sponsor large national events and are a wealth of information about the things that may interest you personally. Having spoken to and verified each of them, (as of this writing) my research assistants and I found them to be very willing to answer questions, and open to assisting people in finding groups in their own area plus offering information on myriad subjects including membership, activities, conventions—anything and everything that make prospective members feel welcome with a sense of belonging. And most importantly, these people understand what it feels like to be floundering in the sea of singles, so they are patient and very understanding. If you are feeling isolated or simply as though you don't know where to turn or how to get started, these fine groups are a wonderful place to start, but it is just the tip of the iceberg.

On a local level, with a tiny amount of effort you can unearth hundreds more. When we started to research opportunities available to singles, we turned up many of the predictable outlets, and many others that were surprising. Instead of throwing up your hands and groping for your remote control, grab your local newspaper or phone book, or visit your local library's reference desk.

Virtually every daily newspaper and certainly every community paper in the country is loaded with events specifically for singles. Check in the community calendar sections, what's happening section or if unsure, just call the paper and ask them where they list events. Then call a friend and make plans to attend some of them. We've all heard the stories of how horrible some single events are. And indeed, some are awful. But many events do get wonderful crowds and new faces that make the experience fun and not at all intimidating. If you're over fifty-five, look for groups that specify that age range. Most ads or event listings mention the age group expected or catered to. It's best to call the number listed and ask questions like: how many people usually attend?, what's the ratio of men to women?, is there a buffet?, an open or cash bar? and most importantly, what are the ages of those attending? This way you can at least make an educated guess about the ones you're interested in. For all the bad PR single dances get, there are thousands of great matches made there every year and just because you go to one that didn't work out, don't discount others.

Usually your main library, is a wonderful source to help you find the books, magazines and articles that list a great many groups and associations – locally and nationally. Also many libraries sponsor hundreds of wonderful events throughout the year themselves—a great way to meet local people who share some of your interests. Ask to be put on their mailing lists as well so you can plan ahead. Outside most libraries or just inside their doors you can find many of the FREE singles newspapers that will specifically list singles organizations in your area.

Another place to find these publications is the local singles bar. Even if you wouldn't ordinarily be caught dead in a bar, go in and visit their cigarette machine. Usually it's jammed with FREE singles publications and flyers hawking local events.

Inside these publications you can find all kinds of events that are *exclusively* for singles, that are right in your own backyard. Some even list trips and weekend get-togethers.

Another great source of events and information is the local bookstore. Many large and small stores now sponsor readings, signings and get-togethers, generally at little or no cost. Many times they attract a large majority of bright interesting people who have common interests, and many, like Barnes and Noble, sponsor their own singles events. An additional source of local singles events are temples and churches, (also Knights of Columbus, YMCA/YWCA, etc.). Sometimes this takes a little leg work, having to call several before you hit pay dirt, but it can yield some great results. Many houses of worship sponsor affiliated singles groups, and many, rent out space to local unaffiliated groups for other events. So do some hotels. If you do take the necessary time, you can uncover several great sources of opportunity.

And lastly, on a local level, many chambers of commerce will have some knowledge of formidable singles groups and organizations in their area. Once you find a group, get your name on their mailing list. There probably will be a good many events you don't want to attend, however, the chances are good that there will be enough events that you'd like to attend that will make the exercise worthwhile.

Another very important point to consider when doing this: men are not the only people you'll meet by joining and exploring some of these alternatives. You'll encounter wonderful, vibrant women just like you, perhaps many with whom you can establish deep friendships and expand your social circle and opportunities locally or nationally. Someone to have dinner with or venture to a singles event with. Even women from other parts of the country should never be discounted. She can visit you and vice versa, further increasing your opportunities and expanding your social circle, (and you can have a ball in the process.) The more people you know and socialize with, the more parties and invitations come your way.

"I can't thank you enough for helping me find Ellen," wrote a female subscriber." When you suggested I call my local travel agencies asking if they arranged trips for singles, I thought it would be a waste of time that was almost confirmed after phoning the first twelve, but thirteen was my lucky number. Ellen, herself single, was in the process of organizing some trips with other singles from our area. I haven't met any eligible men this way, but Ellen and I have become great friends. She and I and about sixteen other people are about to leave for Hong Kong in three weeks. That accomplishes another of my lifelong dreams. I can't believe I didn't think of doing this myself all those years I complained about not having anyone to travel with."

Finding others to vacation with, go to dinner with or to add to the circle of friends you can attend events with, is easier than it looks. It just takes a little work and perseverance, but the rewards are tremendous. Ask yourself this question: If it doesn't involve meeting men have I cut myself off from it? Focusing our attention solely on finding someone of the opposite sex creates a horrible pressure that makes us do dumb things, like quitting a class we enjoy just to be near the phone in case someone calls or hanging out at the local bar just because we don't know where else to turn. And the by-product of this behavior? Sometimes this causes a pressure making us act desperate (I hate that word), and it shows. Other women pick up on it, men pick up on it, thus making us feel more isolated and confused. "I don't waste my time going out with a bunch of women," said Marcia, a fifty-one year old former New Yorker and the bachelorette we named Ms. Anti-Congeniality. "I'm looking for a man."

"Would you even consider the possibility," I said smiling, "that going out with a group of women might give you the opportunity of running into a group of men?"

"Oh," came the *only single word answer* this woman probably ever uttered.

It's attitude and opportunity that will catapult you towards your ultimate goal. The following pages will offer you some of the latter, the rest of the book will give you food for thought on tweaking the former. And one last thing to consider: if you can't find a great group that suits you—start one!

Determination is the mother of luck.
—Ben Franklin

Organizations

ART LOVERS EXCHANGE

Organized in 1985, ALX was created for the "single professional with high aesthetic sensibilities in search of compatible companions with whom to share interests, cultural pursuits and perhaps the rest of your life," offers their membership letter. A national organization for the single art, music, theater, dance, literature, film, photography and crafts lover, they sponsor group social events, parties, gallery visits and discussion groups in addition to a monthly bulletin, *The Easel* which contains a listing of all members of the opposite sex with a twenty-fiveword description of each. A full profile is then available for a two dollar fee and contact after that is via phone or mail. A new members brief description is circulated upon payment of dues: thirty-eight dollars for six months, forty-eight dollars for one year. For information write: Art Lovers Exchange, PO Box 265, Bensalem, PA 19020 or call 800-342-5250.

CONSCIOUSNESS CONNECTION

An organization established in 1989, they are dedicated to those "exploring the frontiers of the mind, body, spirit and planet," says their brochure. Members spread across the U.S., Canada and some foreign countries "share ideas, inspirations and perhaps find a life together. Although members interests are diverse, they center around personal growth, spirituality, metaphysics (astrology, numerology, etc), healing and global consciousness," through correspondence and friendship with the possibility of dating. Membership: six-months, forty-nine dollars/one-year, seventy-nine dollars. Monthly newsletter only twenty-nine dollars. Members are able to advertise their businesses in a free marketplace, place messages to other members in the bulletin board and find out about events via the newsletter. Included with the newsletter are listings for all members of the opposite sex (sixty-five word self-description). If someone raises your consciousness you may request their two-page Life Profile (two dollars each), which every member completes and can then contact them via phone or mail. A membership packet and information can be obtained by writing: 2001 E. Lohman, Suite 110-313, Las Cruces, NM 88001.

COMMITTEE FOR SINGLE ADOPTIVE PARENTS, INC

The organization has existed since 1973 as an information service to prospective and actual single adoptive parents, but they are not an agency. They do provide a source list included in the eighteen dollars, two-year membership listing the agencies with adoptable children open to single applicants. Each source lists briefly the description of children available (age, sex, ethnic background, etc), estimated time and cost. Additionally, they provide information and assistance such as helping you locate and join an adoptive parent support organization in your area. They also publish *The Handbook For Single Adoptive Parents* revised in 1992 for fifteen dollars. For information write: PO Box 15084, Chevy Chase, MD 20825

THE GODDESSESS

A New York based social network formed in 1987 by Nancy Esposito. The primary focus of the group is holding several monthly singles dances and events for "Big, beautiful women and the men who love them," says their newsletter's slogan. The national newsletter offers free personals to members which includes men looking for the larger lady and for the big, beautiful lady herself. Membership is twenty-five dollars annually. For information write: The Goddesses, PO Box 1008, J.A.F. Station, New York, NY 10116 or call (718) 456-9119. For a Free Newsletter send a SASE (#10).

INSTITUTE OF SINGLE DYNAMICS

Founded in 1983, Don Davidson is a charming man who provides churches with assistance in developing and improving ministry programs offered to single adults. A good resource of church groups throughout the U.S., they publish a newsletter, fifteen dollars for the year. For information call: (816) 763-9401 or write: PO Box 11394, Kansas City, MO 64112.

JEWISH SINGLES

Although there is no cohesive national organization that we discovered, there are literally tens of thousands of smaller groups. The JEWISH FEDERATION recommends picking-up a local Jewish newspaper. Most contain listings of local groups and events. Also temples, Jewish community service programs and the local Federation offices are other good sources to check.

NATIONAL ASSOCIATION TO ADVANCE FAT ACCEPTANCE

Founded in 1969, NAAFA is a non-profit human rights organization dedicated to improving the quality of life for fat people. With over fifty local chapters and a newsletter NAAFA works to eliminate discrimination based on body size and provide tools for self-empowerment through public education, advocacy and member support. They have sixteen special interest groups including a singles organization. NAAFA has a yearly convention in a different city and publishes brochures and pamphlets about myriad subjects that concern fat people. They also have an optional NAAFA Date; a computer dating program for members of all sizes and size preferences. They can be reached by phoning: (916) 558-6880 or writing: PO Box 188620, Sacramento, CA 95818.

NAAFA - SINGLES SPECIAL INTEREST GROUP

Holds meetings four times a year at the annual NAAFA conventions in the Spring, Fall, regular convention and also at the Holiday happenings in December. They are split between the west and east coasts. Coordinator Deidra Daley says "members are both thin and fat. The thin person who prefers a fat partner is just as welcome. Our members range in age from twenty-three through seventy and are from all parts of the country. We publish *Single Times*, a quarterly newsletter that has stories and articles of specific interest to the heavy individual with more emphasis on living single successfully, not just focusing on finding a mate. A fat single faces different challenges than their thin counterpart," says Daley. The newsletter also features personal ads from members looking for a companion. Membership is twelve dollars a year and includes the newsletter. For membership information write: 25 E Hoyle St., #112, Norwood, MA 02062, Att: Diedra Daley, Coordinator or call her at: (617) 769-9684.

NATIONAL ASSOCIATION OF CHRISTIAN SINGLES

They provide an uplifting publication called *Today's Single*, a newspaper with a 10,000 circulation of unmarried, divorced, and widowed adults. Says publisher John Fisco, "we inspire, inform, and support Christian singles. We support the theory that all believers are first class citizens in the sight of God and that all persons should be equal without respect to their marital status." They also sponsor a yearly Christian singles conference. To get your name on their mailing list call (414) 344-7300 or for a Free sample of the newspaper write to: 1933 W. Wisconsin Ave. Milwaukee, WI. 53233.

NORTH AMERICAN CONFERENCE OF SEPARATED AND DIVORCED CATHOLICS

"You have to heal yourself of your last relationship, before you can enter into another relationship that will last," offered director Dorothy Levesque. Offering support and comfort, they assist in the formation of new groups; develop programs for existing groups; disseminate information. Emphasis is on lay ministry: those with similar experiences aiding each other. They organize workshops, retreats, educational and training programs, and experiential opportunities, plus they hold a large national conference each year where individuals can socialize, attend seminars and various presentations. Individuals looking for activities locally are referred to approximately 600 similar groups throughout the country. A subscription only quarterly magazine called Jacob's Well is also available. For details write: 80 St. Mary's Dr. Cranston, RI. 02920 or call: (401) 943-7903

PARENTS WITHOUT PARTNERS, INC.

This is an international, nonprofit membership organization devoted to the welfare and interests of single parents and their children. Over 500 chapters and 85,000+ members throughout the U.S. and Canada. 65% female/35% male. All chapters run programs balanced among three areas: Educational, family and adult social/recreational activities. They publish *The Single Parent* magazine which is free to members plus *PWP Insider* a supplement to the magazine that keeps members informed about PWP activities. Members are also invited to participate in the annual convention full of social events, workshops, seminars and youth programs. Yearly memberships range from twenty-five to forty dollars, depending upon the chapter. For more information or to be directed to a chapter in your area call: (800) 637-7974 or write: 401 North Michigan Ave., Chicago, IL 60611-4267.

SINGLE BOOKLOVERS

Started in 1970 by Bob Leach, a widower with three children, to provide a means for unattached, like-minded men and women to get acquainted in a dignified way. "That same year he married me," says Ruth Leach. "A divorcee with four children, I shared his enthusiasm for the organization and it's purpose." With about 1500 members nationwide they provide a newsletter with a literary discussion, bulletin board, book excerpts and mini-two-line profiles of members plus get-togethers open to all on a local level. Interested parties may request the full page profile of members who spark their interest. Membership is fifty-four dollars for the year. A free packet of information on the club is available by calling (610) 358-5049 or writing to: Box 117, Gradyville, PA 19039.

SINGLE DOG LOVERS ASSOCIATION

"When you find someone who loves you, they won't necessarily love your dog. Our organization takes the worry out of that," mused Susie Arndorfer, president of the five year-old organization. Membership which is twenty dollars for six months or thirty dollars for a year includes the bimonthly newsletter with a veterinarian's corner column and profiles of dog-loving members throughout the U.S. The initial contact is through the newsletter, then by mail. All personal information is kept confidential until the two parties agree. For information call: (412) 530-7149. For a Free sample newsletter, information and an application write: 179 Corry Rd. Slippery Rock, Pa. 16057.

SINGLE GOURMET

Founded in 1980, they now have fifteen chapters throughout the U.S., Canada and one in England. "Our objective," says Arthur Fischer, director, "Is to offer single men and women the opportunity to meet each other over a good meal. A choice of several dinners per month and trips throughout the year all center on good food, in an atmosphere conducive to great conversation." A monthly chapter newsletter lists choices and prices generally from twenty-five to seventy-five dollars per meal depending upon the restaurant. Membership is seventy-five dollars for the first year; forty dollar renewals. Non-members are welcomed as guests of members. (It's best to check each local group's policy.) Members have reciprocal membership throughout all chapters: Chicago: (312) 772-3535, Houston, TX (713) 621-7003, Los Angeles: (310) 271-7088 Minneapolis/St. Paul, MN (612) 731-8722, Monmouth City, NJ (908) 290-7447, Nassau/Suffolk Counties, NY (516) 674-6186 Norfolk, VA (804) 623-0687, New York, NY (212) 980-8788, Orange County, CA (714) 854-6552, Philadelphia: (215) 238-1448, Richmond, VA (804) 740-4710, San Diego, CA (619) 238-4300, Sarasota, FL (813) 349-0600. In Canada: Montreal, QB (613) 737-7528, Ottawa, ONT (613) 737-7528, Victoria, BC (604) 383-4279. London, Eng. (071) 243-8699. To write: 133 E. 58th St, NY, NY 10022.

SINGLES IN AGRICULTURE

Founded in 1986, this non-profit organization is comprised of single men and women eighteen years and above who own or work on a farm or who have an agricultural background, or currently working in an agriculture related field. "There are twelve state groups mostly in the Midwest," said former board member Franklin Cook, also a founding member. "We work to enrich the lives of members through a friendship correspondence program. Basically a directory of members interesting in meeting each other. The office will forward the letters for one dollar to protect the privacy of the individual. We also sponsor at least two annual events. A camp-out and annual dinner, open to everyone. The organization offers educational, recreational and social events within the state chapters as well," he said. Their newsletter, *Over The Back Fence* is twenty-five dollars quarterly. The membership directory is thirty-five dollars a year. For information on membership and how the organization works write: Box 7, Pearl City, IL 61062 or call (815) 443-2002.

SENIOR MASTERS

Started in 1980, this is a group of senior citizens (15,000 members) who are of retirement age but are "not yet ready to call it quits." Encouraging seniors to stay active by volunteering or working in an area that interests them. Provides inspiration, direction, information, and ideas about activities; updates members on discounts available to seniors.

For two dollars, they will mail a booklet with information on the organization. Write to: 77 Leland Farm Rd. Ashland, MA 01721 or call (508) 881-8052.

SINGLE MOTHERS BY CHOICE

A national non-profit organization founded in 1981 by Jane Mattes, a psychotherapist, a single mother by choice and author of a Random House book by the same name. The primary purpose is to provide support and information for women who have chosen or are considering single motherhood. Members throughout the U.S. and Canada network with each other, share resources and information on both a local and national level. Several times a year they offer full-day workshops (fifty dollars) for those thinking about the possibility. "Typically a career woman in her thirties or forties," says Mattes, "many of us discovered we could no longer wait for marriage before starting our families. Most preferring to bring a child into the world with two loving parents, but while there is a lifetime to marry, nature isn't so generous in allotting childbearing years. Single mothers by choice is Plan B. Many of our members come into our organization thinking 'yes, this is what I want to do,' and many change their mind. We support them either way." First year membership is forty-five dollars which includes a subscription to the quarterly newsletter or it can be ordered separately for twenty dollars. A full information packet can be obtained by calling (212) 988-0993 or writing: PO Box 1642, Gracie Station, New York, NY 10028.

SINGLES NETWORK

A recognized special interest group of American Mensa, Ltd., the high IQ society, Singles Network is a forum to facilitate the establishment of friendships and romantic relationships for members who have a verified "IQ score of around 132 or higher," through their monthly newsletter. Members are able to write a mini-bio which appears in the newsletter along with information where they may be contacted. They also are able to participate in the on-going discussions of various topics. Dues are twenty-one dollars per year to U.S. addresses, thirty dollars for Canada. For information write: Singles Network, PO Box 41, Palisades, NY 10964-0041 or by calling (914) 359-4607. For a free membership brochure on MENSA call 1-800-66-MENSA, Dept. 9898 or to take an at-home test to see if you qualify send $12 to Mensa, Dept. 9898, 2626 E. 14th St, Brooklyn, NY 11235-3992.

SINGLE PARENT RESOURCE CENTER

Is a non-profit organization with multi-purposes. They provide many direct services to single parents in the New York area, and also refer single parents across the U.S. to local groups (if there are any) in their own area. Says public relations director Suzanne Jones, "we don't want to mislead anyone by saying we have access to a huge infrastructure of groups in all areas, but we do have knowledge of a network of approximately 400 groups throughout the U.S. By providing single parents access to organizations that offer information and support, they feel less isolated and less alone." Additionally, they assist individuals interested in establishing their own local groups and offer materials, manuals, brochures and training. For information send a SASE (#10) to 141 W 28th St. Suite 302 - New York, NY 10001 - Att: Suzanne Jones or call (212) 947-0221.

TALL CLUBS INTERNATIONAL

Started in 1938 by Kaye Sumner Einfeldt a Disney cartoonist for the Seven Dwarfs, this club has grown to fifty-seven chapter throughout the U.S. and Canada with twenty others internationally. Membership vice president, Nellie Perkins works with prospective members to find groups locally for them or she'll assist in helping them create their own. "We're primarily a social group. Each chapter has their own newsletter and runs their own monthly events like informal dinners, dances, brunches, picnics, theme parties and sporting events like bowling and volleyball, plus weekends where local groups invite members from other chapters. We list those events in our monthly newsletter to the chapters," she said. Members must be at least twenty-one years old and women must be 5'10" tall and men must be 6'2". Chapter memberships range from ten dollars per year to fifty dollars, with the majority being twenty-five dollars. Once a year there is a national convention (always 4th of July weekend) and a pre-convention weekend. For full details call (800) 521-2512 or write: 100 Spruce Dr., Yukon, OK 73099, att: Nellie Perkins.

The twenty national organizations mentioned are wonderful places to start, however, there are zillions more locally. There is also a wonderful publication called the *Encyclopedia of Associations*, updated annually, that can be found at your local library's reference desk. In it are thousands of organizations that run the gamut from political, recreational, social and crafts, gardening and social welfare... and everything imaginable in between. A few hours spent with a pad and paper, (you can't check the volumes out) will net you many, many groups that would be delighted to have you as a member and that you'd probably enjoy exploring. Remember, even if it isn't specifically for singles, you'll most likely meet a wealth of wonderful social contacts, and you never know who they'll know. One thing is for sure, you'll be out and enjoying yourself and you'll be expanding your social opportunities.

THE CATHOLIC CLUB— SPARKS SERVICES

Providing an opportunity for unmarried Catholics to make friends by mail, nationwide. Members (1000-1500) are from all 50 states including Puerto Rico, Guam, Canada and Mexico. Not a dating service, the club exists as a source of friendship, although marriages have resulted. Annual fee: $35. Those wanting male/female friendships are sent a listing of opposite sexed members. Members may list their names, addresses or code numbers ($5 additional) and are sent new contacts bimonthly and a quarterly newsletter. Write: Cassie Sparks, PO Box 872, Troy, NY 12181.

THE SAILING SINGLES

Providing singles an opportunity to enjoy sailing with other singles, this service is open to experienced sailors and novices alike. Sailboats from 36 feet are chartered, eliminating cost of hotels and meals. Provisioning (including captains and crew) is provided. Sailing packages w/travel can be arranged. Cruise the British Virgin Isles, St. Martin, Antigua, or Tahiti. Bareboat cruises in the Bahamas, Leeward and Windward islands and several Mediterranean locations also available. Singles wishing to be matched with other singles having similar tastes in destinations, preferences (smoking/non-smoking) and experience can be accommodated. Write: PO Box 901676, Kansas City, MO 64190 or call: (816) 587-6666.

Chapter 8
Being Who You Really Are

This chapter discusses the importance of honesty in a relationship. How many of us have ever behaved differently because we wanted to impress someone? Of course we all have, and in little dribs and drabs it's certainly not harmful. Sometimes it's even helpful. You fudge a little on a resume in order to get the job, and once you have it, you are perfectly capable of doing it. Sometimes imagining ourselves being slimmer helps us to diet. Dreaming of a backyard pool gives us the incentive to work harder to get one. Positive visualization is a wonderful tool. If you think yourself able, you are. If you think you can, you will. But there is a fine line between giving yourself positive reinforcement and blatantly painting a picture of yourself as someone you are not and then having to live up to it.

People say, "I never do that," yet almost all of us are guilty of it at some point... or victims of it. "I was dating a girl for a year and a half and it was going great," said a thirty-five year old Manhattanite. "I really thought this was the girl I was going to marry. It was wonderful. We seemed to be on the same wavelength about almost everything. We liked the same music, the same foods, we even shared a love of baseball... or so I thought. On our fourth date, she brought over a checked table cloth and a picnic basket filled with all the things you'd find at a ball park: hot dogs, popcorn, cold beer; it was so cute. She spread the cloth out on my carpet in front of the TV and we watched a Yankee game. Complete with whooping and hollering. On my birthday she even got us box seats. We went to the game and had a wonderful time. Then around our first anniversary, things started to change. Suddenly she wasn't interested in baseball anymore. She'd go into the bedroom to watch a movie while I watched the game. When I played my rock'n roll tapes, she wanted to hear Anita Baker. And don't think I wasn't interested in compromising, I was. I went with her to antique shows and for romantic walks. But she started to become resentful and nasty when I watched baseball. We'd get into fights every time I'd sit down to watch a game. What I discovered was she really wasn't into baseball at all. In fact, she didn't like my music either. She became who she thought *I wanted* her to be. Now I feel kind of betrayed, I don't think I could trust her anymore. What a waste of time, hers and mine."

Truth and honesty in a relationship is a precursor to trust and intimacy. And it's not like choosing from a Chinese take-out. You can't pick one from column A and one from Column B. You must have them all if a relationship is to grow, deepen, mature and succeed in the long-term.

"I really love him and now he won't even speak to me," wept a forty-four year old beauty. "I didn't lie to him to deceive him, I did it because I knew if I told him how old I really was, he wouldn't take the time to get to know me. He found out when a meddlesome "friend" spilled the beans and now he's furious. Nothing will calm him down. I knew how much he wanted kids, and he feels I deceived him and that he could never trust me again. I thought he was falling so deeply in love with me that it wouldn't matter. But he just packed and left; the whole thing took less than thirty-six hours, and he was gone and won't return any of my calls."

I have gotten the same story from countless single moms who virtually tell their life story to the new men in their lives omitting only a small detail: their kids. This strategy is the superhighway to despair, unlike the message we get from the

TASTER'S CHOICE commercial. After being confronted with his love interest/neighbor's young adult son, he calls and asks, "So, what else have you forgotten to tell me?" Her sensuous toothy smiled reply? "Volumes." The commercial suggests intrigue on the part of the man. That might get you to watch their next commercial or buy the coffee, but in real life, it can lead to disaster. When you meet someone whom you think you can care for, you have two choices. Be honest about who you are and face the possibility that yes, he may bolt if there's something he's not comfortable with or wait until he discovers it and bolts down the road when you are deeply in love with him. The initial rejection might sting, the subsequent rejection can drain the blood from your veins. If something superficial, like a few years or whether you're a natural blonde, will bother him at the beginning, he's a jerk. And if he is, what makes you think he won't be a jerk further into the relationship? What makes you think he can be converted into Mr. Sensitive along the way? The only difference is whether you're mildly pissed or a basketcase. However, if it's some fundamental preference he has (like wanting his own children, or never wanting any, or raising them in a specific religion, or a love for a sport, hobby, etc.), which conflicts with your preference and you overtly lie to show instant compatibility, you're the jerk. He has the same *right to know* that you have.

"I think the thing that turns me off the most," said Isaac, a forty year old publishing executive, "is when a woman tries to deceive you from the very beginning, but in her eyes it's not doing anything wrong. When I met Erica, she spent the whole first evening putting down other women who she said were clingy and needy and who built their wholes lives around men. She convinced me she was confident and self-assured. After about six dates, I saw her drive down my street to see if I was home. She started questioning me, and then when I broke it off, she tries to convince me it's because I led her on and I'm threatened by a confident woman. I wanted to tell her it was because she was the personification of what she said she despised, but I didn't want to destroy what little self-esteem she did have. Women think men are so thick they can't see what's really going on. In some cases that may be true, but in most cases I think we know plenty—we just choose to keep our mouths shut."

Why are we afraid to be who we are? Studies say it's because we don't think we're good enough. It's our own sense of self-esteem that has been the root of many a relationship breakdown. For most of us, feeling worthy is a constant struggle. For all the advances women have made, there is still the nagging fear that something is missing. The feelings of inadequacy and self-doubt accompany much of our success as evidenced by the hundreds of self-esteem books that flood the market. I am not a psychologist, and I don't profess to be able to pinpoint from whence these feelings came—the reasons we are beset with them, or to tell you how to exorcise them. As evolved as I believe I am, as far as I have come in my career and hopefully in my emotional life, I too still wrestle with the same demons from time to time. Where do these feelings come from? Even the Bible in all its infinite wisdom might very well be the most chauvinistic document ever written. In Genesis 2:18-22, its message to women is loud and clear: "For even before God thought of creating woman, He created all the beasts of the field and birds of the sky and brought them to Adam, the first man, for him to name, and from which to find one suitable helper." Only after none was found did God create woman.

And women wonder where this feeling of "unworthiness" came from??????? Perhaps we are still paying penance for that apple fiasco long ago, or we've simply put too much on our plate. Who knows? What I do know is the power self esteem (or the lack of it) has on the dynamics of a relationship. Now that you're aware of the places to find someone who will adore you exactly as you are, *you* just have to learn to do the same.

Chapter 9

"A" You're Adorable, "B" You're So Beautiful

The Key to Unlocking Your Desirability

Men duked it out over Audrey Hepburn as Holly Golightly in *Breakfast at Tiffany's*; they swarmed Elizabeth Taylor as Gloria Wanderous in *Butterfield 8*; Arlene Dahl enthralled them as Eileen Percy in *Three Little Words*; Gertrude Lawrence swam in a sea of gentlemen callers as Amanda Wingfield in *The Glass Menagerie*, and, lest we forget, the fair Vivian Leigh as Scarlett O'Hara in *Gone With The Wind*—she not only was constantly surrounded by interested men, but, in the end, she got the most desirable of them all, old *"I don't give a damn,"* Rhett.

These are just characters in the movies, you say. That's not real life, you declare. Say it isn't so, rings the collective squeal. We've all seen women who simply slay men with the bat of an eyelash. Not only are those fictional characters reflective of real life, many of them were taken from real life.

Countless times we have seen a woman we deem less attractive literally swamped by men at the company picnic. *What the hell could she be saying to them?* we ask ourselves. *Reciting Mickey Mantle's batting average or Billy Martin's winning coaching strategies??* Or how about the office Christmas party? *Wasn't that Plain Jane, Quasi-Modo's look-alike, dancing with the resident stud? What'd she do, drop a mickey in his Asti-Spumante?*

What are their collective secrets? What is it they know that you don't? How can a woman turn on charm that will make men *want* to sweep her off her feet?

Insuring Desirability—What Works, is a list compiled via careful observation and interviews with women deemed irresistible by men, and also, from men who spoke about the kind of women who consistently make their heads spin. This chapter uncovers the secrets (which really are not secrets at all) about just what it is these women do that instinctively works.

#1/ A WOMAN WHO TRULY LIKES MEN IS IMMENSELY ATTRACTIVE TO THEM

A handsome thirty-four year old bachelor who heads a multi-million dollar eyewear company describes that kind of charisma as, "a woman who doesn't take herself too seriously. Someone who can laugh easily and who seems comfortable when she's talking to me. Not stiff or calculating like she's trying to come up with clever repartee to captivate my interest." His tennis-pro friend George, a tan, lean forty-five year old *hunk* by anyone's standards, agreed. "A woman who *likes* men is just naturally secure around them. She isn't worried about proving how smart she is, how clever a conversationalist she can be. She just chats, naturally. She doesn't have to look like a super model either. Women who like themselves and are therefore comfortable around men, exude that something special and are just naturally attractive."

"If you see a crime in progress," said a thirty-eight year old hair stylist for a chic New York salon, "you're supposed to call the police, right? I saw one of my roommates steal my other roommate's boyfriend right in front of her and anyone else who was watching. We were all having dinner and talking, but Allison just seemed to be on his wavelength. Everything *we* said seemed contrived although it wasn't. Allison just seemed to go from one subject to the next with such ease. He seemed captivated by her. Allison isn't a man-stealing hussy, don't get me wrong, she just has that certain something that reduces men to

Silly Putty in her hands. I wouldn't bring my man within 60 feet of her. And it's not like she'd walk away with the crown at a Miss America pageant either. She does keep herself trim, but she's just sort of ordinary."

"I knew it too," said the now boyfriendless Deanna. "You just had to see the expression on Don's face every time he made eye contact with her. He kind of locked eyes and grinned boyishly. Instead of throwing her out on her ear, I'm trying to figure out what it is that she just does."

What she *does* so much better than most is something very, very simple. She really *likes* men, not just as potential mates. She likes them and just sees them as *people*. This kind of woman is not trying to captivate them or seduce them (as some women we've all seen) she just likes them.

Ever get together with a bunch of single women to shoot the breeze? "Why did the man cross the road?" a gorgeous twenty-four year old blonde nursing student asks her equally beautiful twenty-six year old friend who shrugs her shoulders.

"Who knows why the hell they do *anything* they do," is the answer, which is followed by laughter, knee slapping and an onslaught of man-bashing war stories. "You've got to see this card my sister sent me," says an attractive thirty year old secretary yanking it out of her purse. The front is a woman holding a smoking gun. The heading reads: "So Many Men." The inside? "so few bullets." More laughter. "Isn't that the truth?" offers the most physically beautiful of the six, "All men lie, cheat and will say and do anything to get what they want. The only good ones are sleeping with each other." More laughs. These women are having a great time, the only problem? It's Saturday night and each one of them would rather be out being wined and dined.

The women like Allison, who *are* out Saturday night being wined and dined, come in all shapes and sizes. The difference is they genuinely *enjoy* the company of men. They may laugh at the jokes, but they don't buy into that man-bashing phenomena—a fascination selling millions of dollars worth of cards.

"But I do like men," you say, *but you just wouldn't trust one.* "But I do like men," you say, *but you just don't think there are any decent ones left.* "But I do like men," you say, *but you think they all have an overblown sense of themselves... or are commitment phobic, or uncommunicative, or schmucks that have to be pointed in whatever direction they walk.*

Remember when all those dumb blonde jokes were being told by everyone who had a working tongue? Sure blondes laughed like everyone else *for a time*. After a while, though, they started to get a tad testy. I think men are getting a tad testy about the man-bashing, and who can blame them? In Chapter Four, I illustrated the effect the Women's Movement was having on relationships. Simultaneous to relationships becoming a casualty of changing roles—men became the butt of our jokes. It was a way for us to vent frustration about the inequality which seemed not to be equalizing fast enough. While the feminists were on the front lines changing the perception, treatment, and injustices perpetrated against women, many of us were firing pot shots of our own: *man-bashing jokes*. We did what we do best. We used our humor to get the point across and still maintain our femininity. Women who bashed men got paid for it and were showered with attention and adoration. Men who bashed insensitive men were exalted to grandiose levels. In the beginning it was funny and purposeful, shocking men who didn't want to be deemed "insensitive" into grocery shopping, laundry and getting the kids out of our hair for some "quality" time in the park.

But somewhere along the way we bought into this, hook, line and sinker as if this were gospel to be indoctrinated right along with the ABC's to our daughters. Is it any wonder some of you feel like this? That's all we hear, that's all we see. Is it any wonder that men subconsciously seem to duck and dodge us in a relationship? They're waiting for us to throw the next punch.

Almost thirty years later, the strides have been incredible, yet we have a long way to go. Laws *have* been changed prohibiting discrimination, women *are* able to achieve personally and professionally. Unfortunately, inequities, *huge* inequities remain. But it has only been thirty years for crying-out-loud. Isn't it unfair to blame every man in the '90s who breathes? I certainly don't want to sound like a bleeding-heart, but men have been laying down their very lives to protect women and children, with little question. There are a million municipal *volunteer* firefighters in this country—99% of them are men. This door is open to women, but how many of us choose to go through it? Indeed, we should rightfully be able to do whatever a man has the opportunity to do, but if we're honest, how many of us really would? For me personally, it's one very different thing to wage war in the boardroom, it's another doing it for real in a foxhole. As genuinely grateful as I am to the feminists who have brought changes allowing me to do what it is I choose to do, that's how deeply grateful and respectful I am of the men and women who have fought to keep me safe from harm while I'm doing it. For years men have been taking life-threatening, mucky, low prestige jobs just because they can earn a higher wage for their families. Roofers, loggers, miners... garbage collectors. Most women still wouldn't work at a great many of the jobs that equality opened the door enabling us to perform.

Years ago, I belonged to the *Anti-Men Haagen Das Appreciation Association.* Fancy name for a group of about ten to fifteen who joined together monthly to vent, commune and support each other. Admission? A pint of your favorite flavor and a war story or two. But that was then. And now? I love to laugh at the jokes and I've used many as spoof cartoons in our magazines, but I am acutely aware of their negative effects as well. Through my research, I have garnered the deepest, most abiding respect, admiration and love for men *as people.* And *please,* don't think I haven't met my share of cads, clods, creeps and cretins. I have. I just haven't let it eclipse my understanding that there are ten times as many wonderful, warm, witty and genuine others out there.

It isn't that most women don't get along with men. I don't

think many women really take the time to truly understand men, and if they do, few are patient enough to interact with them on their level, which is neither above nor below ours, but just different. Growing up with a mom who always referred to my dad as a Martian, I watched my brother and dad whoop and holler watching sporting events and always felt like an outsider with my face pressed up to the glass. I watched my parents' parties from a distance—the men massed in the living room as the women flocked to the kitchen.

But as I grew up, I was the one who ended up in the living room with the men, *where I listened and learned*. They weren't talking in some strange alien tongue, nor were conversations peppered solely with sports trivia or complaints about the "old-ball-and-chain." They talked about women, cars, houses, wives, work, kids ... just like the women. The difference was they also talked politics, world affairs, taxes and other issues impacting us. In the kitchen, it was sniffles, diaper rash, recipes and the best stain removers. But back then, the scope of our lives was different–men were out in the world, so their conversations were more universal. Women were in the home and their conversations were centered there. It wasn't that men arrived on earth via a spaceship. Today, as women, our lives are more global and so is our conversation. Men are being irked by the pesky port stain that Wisk won't shout out. We see the shift, but some still prefer to harbor the Martian theory.

Meaningful relationships (non-work related) with men do not have to be predicated on either sex or sports. You don't have to shake-your-booty in front of them or fix cars to precipitate communication with a man, but that's how most women have been taught to approach them. It's not that at all. You simply have to *like* men. Not pretend commonalities, but genuinely *like* them enough to become comfortable around them. And when you do, it shows.

The second most powerful aphrodisiac, save for running by naked with a sign that says "come on", is *Self Confidence* ....

2/ SELF CONFIDENCE.
A WOMAN WHO FEELS GOOD ABOUT HERSELF ATTRACTS MEN LIKE BEES TO NECTAR

I know this whips right back to the self-esteem issue but 85% of the men interviewed mentioned self-confidence as the first thing they become attracted to (after the two most superficially obvious). "The woman I'm looking for exudes confidence more from having a full and interesting life, rather than simply nice packaging," says a forty-five year old business attorney from St. Catherines, Ontario. He also made a lasting impression when he said, "Packaging will surely get me to turn my head, but if that's all there is, it certainly won't keep it bent in that direction very long."

A twenty-seven year old teacher who works with autistic children in western Pennsylvania put it this way: "I'm attracted first by physical appearance. I'd be lying if I said otherwise. But I've seen plenty of physically beautiful women who had little to contribute beyond appearance. There was no presence, if you know what I mean. They were the sum total of what they looked like. Not that they weren't intelligent, but they were so concerned with their hair, their make-up or outfit, that it *took away* from their desirability. They couldn't relax, it's as if *they* didn't think their own worth extended much beyond appearance. That's lack of self-confidence and at least for me, it's a huge turn-off."

"Dear Mindi," the letter started. "I feel like a complete fool for even wanting to write this letter, more so for mailing it. You see I am a doctor with a very successful practice in Long Island, New York. My practice employs ten people and two associates, each believing I could climb Mount Kilimanjaro if I set my mind to it. There's no medical dilemma I can't figure out, no question from the office staff I can't answer and no professional stride I can't make. What I can't seem to do is find a significant other." And please don't think I haven't made my share of attempts, I have," Lydia wrote. "From a $5,000 professional matchmaker to $2,200 for a local dating service to a personal ad in a prestigious NY magazine. Nothing happened, nada, zippo. I've enclosed a picture, I'm not Miss Universe but I don't bay at the moon either."

Lydia the doctor is certainly a force to reckon with in her own environment, out of it she flounders. Interacting at her office she questions very few of her decisions, interacting with men she questions them all. When we talked privately, she admitted she never really feels comfortable with men, often adjusting her position over and over, smoothing her hair and patting her outfit when she first meets them. Then she does things for them like cooking, buying little presents or cards, what I call tending them. "I guess in a strange way it goes back to my mother's reaction to my father coming home. The house would be cleaned, the dinner on the stove but when she heard his car door slam in the driveway, she jumped up like a crazy woman, no matter what she was doing. She'd run to the kitchen and start puttering. She could have worked her fingers to the bone and just sat down but she'd never let Dad catch her "relaxing" when he walked through that door. I guess she was trying to justify her day, or her worth. I vowed that I'd never be like that. I suppose that's what propelled me into becoming a doctor. I make almost $200,000 a year and knew I'd never have to justify my worth, but I guess some of what my mom felt rubbed off on me anyway."

Since there was no high school class on finding a man, no book on how to behave once we get one, or even a manual on how to pick out the one who'll make us happy. Most of us learned by *watching*. And who did we watch? Our parents. So the degree to which our parents' idiosyncrasies have caused our own uneasiness is relevant only to the point at which we recognize from whence these feelings came. The bottom line is to get healthy and keep those things from having an adverse effect on us now. Men are attracted to *Lydia the capable professional* and several stick around for several dates or short-term relationships, but when she lapses into behavior that reveals an enormous lack of confidence, they exit.

So what should we do, short of humming "I Am Woman" in our heads all day? All of us have our strengths and weaknesses and similarly things we're very confident about and things we're not. One of the so called "secrets" to attracting men is to become more secure. And to do that you can read some of the wonderful books on the subject and practice what they preach, and you can also find a therapist you trust and work things out professionally. Simultaneously, you can aim for *projecting* a self-confident, well-rounded, totally together image. Just close your eyes for a minute and envision yourself as the person you want to be. Come on, we've all done it. I bought this slinky black dress for my twentieth reunion and I remember thinking, *if I were only thirty pounds thinner how incredible it would look*. Well, in my head I envisioned myself in that dress, only in a slightly thinner body. (Who am I kidding, thirty pounds is *slightly??*) But it worked. I felt voluptuous, sexy and *confident*, which was key. I'm not suggesting the creation of superwoman, or a duplicitous existence, simply a persona who says, "I like who I am, I'm comfortable with who I am, I am assured in any situation, I have a full, stimulating life on my own and you as a man would enrich my life, not *establish nor confirm* it." By projecting that aura, you immediately put men at ease. You make them instantly comfortable and attracted to you. They look and say, "This is a woman who's her own person. She won't suck the life out of me trying to make herself whole, she already is."

"My whole marriage was one enormous responsibility for me," said Mark a thirty-two year old copier technician from Los Angeles. "I bought into the 'two halves make a whole' concept, but that's bull. Two *wholes* are what propels a relationship towards growth. Today, the first barometer I use in determining if a relationship will proceed is discerning if the woman *needs* me because she cares for me and I add a dimension to her life or she needs me to *complete* it. I run from the latter."

This is where number two and three fuse into one another and it's a fine line that separates them.

3/ HOLD A LITTLE BACK
AND RETAIN YOUR POWER (IDENTITY)

Many of us may think that what Mark says he's looking for is who we already are, yet the men we meet may be getting a different impression; primarily because we slowly become somebody *else* once we end up in a quasi-relationship. It's not a conscious thing though, like, *Today I'm in love, tomorrow I'll be a drivel*. One of my closest friends has a sister she is always talking to me about. The sister is the COO (chief operating officer) of a multi-million dollar travel company. "She asked me," my friend said, "if I'd mind coming over to her house Wednesday, instead of going to the movies as we had planned for over a week. I got pissed. She does this to me all the time. When I didn't immediately agree, she got that *look* on her face. The one that means 'he' is supposed to call. 'You don't always have to be there,' I said with little or no impact. 'I know,' she answers, 'but it's a new relationship and I'm a little anxious.' This from a captain of industry who can reduce people to rubble with a stare. My sister gets like that with every man she starts to become involved with. She gets herself tied to the tracks. She acts like a demented damsel in distress."

"He," and the string of incredible "he's" before him all met June through business. They *all* were attracted to the strong, confident extraordinarily capable woman she really is. In the beginning of all her relationships, the men have to work around her incredibly busy schedule just to talk to her. After two or three months of intermittent dates, when she becomes emotionally attached, she begins bending like a willow tree in the wind to be accessible to them. *What she's doing is giving up all her power*—always being available, always giving up her outside interests, waiting to hear from or be with "him." Inadvertently appearing weak, or clingy or needy—just the *opposite* of why the men were attracted to her in the beginning. What this behavior does is force men farther and farther away from her. The effect she hoped it would have is endearing her to them. It doesn't.

This odd phenomenon is what most women are still the most confused over. We're aloof. He comes on like Schwarzkopf charting Desert Storm. We're still aloof, but beginning to put down our wall. He presses. We're still wary... *What's his motive?* He presses harder. We relent and return his feelings. He bolts like the gopher who sees his shadow. I call it the one-step-forward-two-step-back screenplay:

ACT I - SCENE ONE: After knowing each other two months he suddenly spills his guts one Thursday night over Moussaka and Ouzo in a Greek restaurant, professing repressed feelings for you.

AHA! I knew it, I knew it, I knew it!!! says your inner voice sounding way too much like Fran Drescher on "The Nanny." *I knew he was in love with me.* I know I'm the only one he can talk to so deeply, who understands him so well. *I'm the one. Meanwhile, you're chewing.*

The savvy, conscious you says, *NO, I'm not gonna leap up on his lap and say, take me I'm yours. NO, I'm not going to the nearest phone and tell my mother to register the china pattern. NO, I'm not going to write my first name with his last on the tablecloth in front of him. I'm simply going to reach out, touch his hand and smile warmly, saying nothing.*

Good move, good move, says you're other Roseanne-like fairy-god voice. He takes you home, kissing you at the door, his passion at depcon 2.

You: "I have to get to the office early tomorrow." Him: "I'll call you tomorrow night."

Minutes after you finish putting a mud mask on your face and cucumber slices over your eyes, the phone rings. (It's only been two hours.) Him: "I had such a good time. I can't stop thinking about you."

ACT II - SCENE TWO: Saturday night. After Moo Shoo pork and a bottle of Sake he takes you home, only this time you let him in. In your living room on the couch, making wild passionate love: Him: "Yes." You: "Yes." Him: "Yes." You: "Yes, yes." Him: "Yes. I don't think I'll ever be able to get enough of you." You: "I'm crazy about you, too. I knew we were right for each other."

SCENE THREE: In the morning you leap out of bed while he's still asleep, put on a natural glow and head for the kitchen. Two napkins that match, orange juice, Special K, Taster's Choice coffee, and a rose you picked from the garden yourself. He stumbles in and pecks at your neck before starting to eat.

You: (looking starry-eyed into his tousled hair) "What do you want to do today?" Him: "I've got to go home and finish a big report for tomorrow." You: (feeling crushed but trying to look cheerful) "I thought we'd go bike riding, stopping at the covered bridge to carve our names in it and have a wild and woolly picnic." Him: "Sounds great, but I can't today," as he eats everything on the table but the rose. You: "Will you call me later?" (the panic/confusion mounting as you watch him gather his clothes) Him: "Yes." (on his way out the door.)

ACT III - SCENE FOUR: Sitting at home for eight hours, you have bisected and dissected every spoken and *unspoken* word of last night's scenario with no less than seven of your closest girlfriends. At five o'clock you can't stand it anymore and drive by his house with two deli sandwiches and an oversized pickle to share. DING DONG. Him: "Oh, hi." You: "I was just driving by and thought you'd be hungry." Him: "I just ate but that was really sweet. I was going to call you but I'm up to my eyeballs in work. I'll call you Monday night."

You go home and call your cronies: *the Monday night poker game is off!*

EPILOGUE: You start watching the clock at 5:01pm, the second it officially becomes Monday night. He doesn't call. This is the most frustrating of all relationship dilemmas. You did nothing wrong, save for waiting by the phone. Yet you feel abandoned and mistrustful of men.

Somewhere between the thrill of the hunt and catching the prey, the hunter gets a little drunk with his own success. It's worse, much worse if during the hunt, the prey flings herself on the spear. As many times as I've queried men about this, there's still no clear cut, official answer—like if you have a sore throat, gargle and take aspirin. What does keep emerging however, is that men *do* enjoy pursuing a self-confident woman. She has her own life and interests (she's not sure he's the one, so she hasn't canceled her dance class yet). She's intriguing (she's holding back, not spilling her guts). She's mysterious (she's keeping her mouth shut till she knows something concrete). And being kept a wee bit off-kilter, the men do fall in love with them—that's the one-step-forward. It's when the woman throws down her arms and totally surrenders or appears to, that the two-step-back rule comes into play. I have cats, and once spotted my big orange Henry, who loves to spend hours at the base of trees trying to catch salamanders, literally beaned by one as it fell off a branch right into Henry's open paws. He just panicked, and ran away. Wasn't that what he was waiting around nine hours for? Imagine the bewildered salamander? He's been up there trying to avoid the jaws of death, and then he makes one wrong move and falls into them and they get scared and run away. Bet he's paying some salamander with a Ph.D., ninety bucks an hour to sort that one out.

It's certainly not that you should play games and withhold how you feel. But it seems the "secret," if you will, is that you must do it in stages. Small, encouraging stages. Men need to feel wanted and appreciated but there's a fine line between that, and clinging and smothering. Men will come forward when they have feelings, but when we go out and pick up honeymoon travel brochures, they back up big time. How far they back up is usually dependent on how many people we have already invited to the wedding, if you know what I mean.

There are two important points here: The first is that you must stay the intriguing, interesting person who made him desire you in the first place. You cannot transfer all your power in the relationship to him. You have an answer machine, possibly a mobile phone. Do not give up your mud wrestling classes or your EST training. He can leave a message or call you later or before. And if he's really interested, you not being there to receive a phone call will not send him running into the arms of another. You are at a pivotal point here. You must create boundaries whereby you'll continue to be desired, respected and admired. You do not want to become Donna the Doormat. You know what happens to doormats. They get walked on. If you genuinely feel this guy has long-term potential, don't ever play games just to leave him hanging; certainly make sure he knows you care, but do so in such a way that you don't look like Donna in his eyes.

The second point is that you must carefully interpret what he *means*. We are sensitive creatures who can sometimes go from zero to sixty like a Jaguar in heat. You may have a man who genuinely cares for and is falling in love with you, but as women, we accelerate what this *means to us*, which can be a very different thing to him; this is not to say that he won't catch up. He might; *if* you don't make him back up so far he falls off the cliff, out of sight. If the relationship doesn't flourish, it's not always because he's a maladjusted rat in man's clothing. "I'm tired of taking the rap on that one," says David, an extremely successful thirty-nine year old corporate attorney. "I know it sounds like I'm a control-freak, but I'm not. I just want to feel like the relationship is moving at a speed I'm comfortable with. It's my experience that women push too fast, not because they're desperate, but because they keep misreading signals and then accelerating what they believe they mean. I'll show a woman I'm dating I care, but then if she takes over and starts recreating the pace. If I'm not comfortable, I'll exit. I know it's hard for women too these days to find a comfortable power balance, but don't they realize that nothing turns a guy off more than when he feels powerless in a relationship? Sometimes the only option open to regain some of the control is to leave."

4/ LEARN TO FLIRT

Flirting is a gentle art that whispers seduction. It's subtle, like locking eyes and softly smiling as he passes. It's not shouting, "Yo, Papa San, over here." Done correctly, it can send signals that can get any (okay, *almost*) any man's attention. Flirting is the way you walk, the way you laugh, the way you run your finger over the tip of your glass and the way you listen. It allows you to exude sensuality without being overt, convey interest without uttering a word and drive men wild without dropping your drawers. In order to fill your dance card, you have to focus on this with the same fervor you do anything else that's important to you. Men need to be encouraged, just not hit on the head. "I can't tell you the electric current that ignites in me when a woman purposefully locks eyes with me," says a forty-eight year old fire chief from Tempe, Arizona. "I sizzle when a woman lightly touches me in conversation. When a woman knows how to flirt it's powerfully attractive. But there is a fine line between flirting and coming on too strong. I've seen so many women who can't seem to tell the difference."

5/ BE HAPPY

"Women who are happy are just more enjoyable to be around," said Chris, a forty-five year old record producer. "I've been out with women who are great in the beginning and then once you get close, boom. You become the sounding board for every rotten thing their ex ever did. You have to hear about every traffic jam, every cruddy thing the boss made them do. It starts becoming a drag just to call and say, 'Hi!' So, I do it less and less until it's no fun at all anymore. And don't think I'm not sensitive and don't want to be supportive. But support is different than being a whipping boy."

Don, a thirty-eight year old civil engineer, agreed. "Men enjoy being around a woman who's happy. Someone like that just makes me feel good and like I don't have to *make* her happy. I've gone with women who say they're happy people; but aren't. Laughing at jokes doesn't mean you're a happy person. Happy comes from within. They don't moan and complain all the time. When a woman does that, I somehow feel like she's making these things my fault, even though intellectually I realize she's not. It makes me feel helpless, because I can't offer solutions. That's why happy, easy-going women are such a turn-on. When you find a woman like that, you can just go about the business of really enjoying each other."

It's simple. You, me, men,..., everyone would much prefer to be around someone who is in a good mood than someone who continually has the weight of the world on his or her shoulders. "You can certainly be there to let someone blow off steam," said Andre, a thirty year old tire company salesman from Omaha, Nebraska. "But a constant barrage of whining, complaining or worse, someone who's constantly looking to be coddled, can bring you down enough that you start to pull away from that person."

So even if Murphy (of rules fame) himself came to live in your house for a weekend, don't bend everyone's ear. Certainly talk to those close to you, but let it go. Don't dwell or drone on. Think about it in reverse. If you were dating some guy who spent the majority of his conversation with you moaning and complaining or who found fault with everyone and everything, he wouldn't be very appealing. Happiness is your most powerful asset. If you're upbeat and happy, men will enjoy being with you.

6/ LAUGHTER IS THE BEST MEDICINE

There is not enough that can be said about the effects of humor. The ability to make someone laugh is an invincible edge. "I love to laugh," said Casey, a twenty-six year old former Marine from Branson, Missouri. A woman who can make me laugh and who can take a joke is incredibly attractive to me. Laughing has gotten me through some of the rough spots in my life and I couldn't imagine being with someone who took everything so seriously."

I met a couple at a cocktail party. He was a successful restauranteur, a handsome, sharp man with tremendous presence. We were talking for quite a while when he looked around and said, "I can't seem to spot my wife. I really want to introduce the two of you." He proceeded to tell me all about this adventurous, off-beat, free-spirit with an incredible sense of humor who still, after eight years of marriage, he can't predict. With that, a rather mousy looking brunette came over and said, "Hi, I'm Susan, Arthur's wife." In the split second between when I looked at her and when we started to talk, I couldn't see the connection. I couldn't fathom that the woman I was looking at could be the same woman he was raving about. But, within four minutes, we were all laughing and I was as captivated by her as he apparently was. Laughter can put a man at ease, it can take the tension out of sticky situations and the feeling it gives can bond someone to you forever. It's human nature to prefer to be around people who make you feel good.

The "secrets" to attracting men and *holding* their attention?

Present yourself as confident, secure and optimistic.

Like men for who they are as people, and display an ease with those around you.

Don't be noticeably preoccupied by what you look like.

Be poised and encouraging, not overly anxious or vulnerable like 'Donna the Doormat'.

Be sanguine and upbeat, not like the weight of the world sits just beneath your head, even if it does.

Chapter 10

The First Date -
Wisdom To Make Sure There's A Second

If finding a man is the contest, sustaining a fulfilling relationship is surely the prize, but you have to get past the first date to do it. Hysterically funny for some and just plain disasters for others, it is a perplexing proposition for most, especially if he never calls again. In accordance with the information proposed in Chapter Nine, I now offer an all important look at things that universally turn men off.

As with all good things, like chocolate and ice cream, too much of them can make you throw up. Once you are aware of the personal power that comes along with the development of the right attitude (self-esteem) and its accompanying desirability, you need to integrate this behavior into your life without becoming a battering ram at a hoedown. You might feel like painting a big red S on your chest, but resist the temptation. As lovely as that red cape might look with your new clogs, you don't have to strain to make people aware. *They'll just know.* We've all been backed into a corner by someone who resembles Cliff, the semi-lovable bar stool warmer in the TV sitcom "Cheers." He knows something about everything and he's got this overwhelming need to *share* this information...*constantly.*

Desirability is something you exude, not broadcast—a natural result of total personality development. But when you feel like you can "leap tall buildings with a single bound," make the jump with grace or you might end up like Humpty Dumpty. You remember the guy, a big, hefty fellow. He sat on a wall, then the egghead had a great fall. All of the King's horses and all of the King's men couldn't put Humpty back together again. What they never told us, was that he was probably *pushed* off by some bug-eyed woman he was boring to death up there. Confidence is power, being an authority on everything is overkill.

RULE #1: NEVER MONOPOLIZE THE CONVERSATION

As anxious as you might be to make sure he sees all your wonderful qualities, you must refrain from making sure you get them all in. "I went out with Samantha the first time and I chose a quiet little Italian place so we could talk and get to know each other. I hardly got a word in," complained twenty-five year old Anthony, a stockbroker from Columbus, Georgia. "She'd ask me a question, but every time I started to give my answer, it seemed to remind her of something in her life and she'd be off again. I really didn't have a good time. I felt like I had a job opening and she was the applicant making sure she really sold herself."

"I'm uncomfortable when a woman asks me direct personal questions on a first date," said John, fifty-three, a San Francisco art dealer. "But what I hate worse is when she feels the need to divulge all her personal information upfront. Sometimes I feel like those women need a shrink, not a date."

"Sometimes, if we're having an easy-conversation, I don't mind being given information about their past." answered Ben, a forty-four year old attorney. "What bothers me is when they out and out brag. Constantly mentioning this possession or that one. I always wonder why they're doing that. Is it to get me to match it, so they think we're on equal footing? Is it to intimidate me into thinking they're wonderful for having achieved it, or is it to validate their own worth? I appreciate a woman who has achieved. I just don't want it rammed down my throat."

On the same subject, thirty-three year old Bob, a land surveyor added. "I never mind telling women things about myself, if the conversation is flowing. But most women want you to know so much about them, they give you their whole life history—illnesses, bad relationships. I *like* to take my time and get to know a woman. I like the discovery period. When they give it all to you up front, it's like there's no challenge."

"The thing that turns me off when it comes to first date conversation," said Robert, a twenty-nine year old auto worker, "is when a woman is so strong-willed and opinionated that she puts down my views. I don't mind healthy disagreements, I just don't like that superior attitude—if an opinion is different from hers it's automatically wrong. The thing I hate worst of all? Is when a woman spreads gossip, especially if she's constantly putting down other people. I just think if she'll tell me so much confidential stuff on the first date when she hardly knows me – what might she be saying about me? I think women who do that, shoot themselves in the foot."

The first date is a provocative, anticipatory time and it's best if you stay a bit mysterious; that's not to say be evasive or withhold conversation, just offer what you need to and bring the conversation back to him. First, this appeals to most men's delight in talking about themselves. Second, it will drive him crazy with desire to know more, calling again for the second date and third. It leaves room for continued discovery—the time you need to determine if you think the guy has long-term potential. Be astute and keep his conversation flowing and *don't be negative*. Men pick up on this much more than we realize and it makes a horrible lasting impression. We end the date feeling great because we got a lot off our chest, believing we planted impressions that dazzled him, and we assume he had just as good a time. The way we find out he didn't? He never calls again. If there's chemistry, keeping your conversation upbeat and on the light side will have him calling for more.

RULE #2: REMEMBER THE ART OF THE COMPLIMENT

Appropriately timed, a compliment will allow you to establish a sense of ease, deepening the rapport you're hoping to establish with your companion. But you must be careful. No one is suggesting you fire compliments like rounds of ammunition. This would not only be highly transparent, it would make your date *uncomfortable*. Exactly opposite of how you want him to feel. Effective compliments focus on the person's appearance, behavior, accomplishments or possessions. "Yo, Bubba, you look hot in those jeans!" won't cut it. Neither will "Yee-ow, look at that rock on your finger. Must be making the big bucks, eh?" You need to slip them in with grace and sophistication. Being specific helps and so does following it up with a question. "You're a wonderful dancer, where did you learn to dance so well?"

Similarly, if you are at the receiving end of a compliment don't downplay what's expressed. "I don't know about women today," said Sam, a forty-three year old barber. "They have this can-do attitude about everything and then when you compliment them on their accomplishments, or even something like their outfit they say, 'What, this old thing?' It makes me feel stupid and also makes them look as though they really don't have any confidence."

If you rebuff someone's compliments enough, he just won't make anymore, believing if you don't think you're worthy, why should he? Just answer by saying, "Thank you, I've had this for years but it still makes me feel good."

Rule #3 - Don't Talk About Past Relationships

Nothing turns a man off faster than being with a woman he barely knows who does nothing but complain about her misfortunes with men or why the other 99% of the male population is pond scum (present company excluded). "I dated Pam a couple of times," said Steve, a very attractive twenty-four year old private fitness trainer. "Every time we went out it'd be going great and then something would remind her of her ex and she launched into a dissertation. I never called her after that and then about a month later we ran into each other at the health club and she says, 'We had such a great time together; how come you stopped calling?' Go figure."

"All I said," offered Allen," was, 'So you were married once.' That set off an explosion of anger and angst about her husband who used her, and lied to her and left her in a lurch. I felt sorry for her, but I'm not looking to rescue someone. I want a woman who's come to grips with her past and is living in the present."

Don't, under any circumstances, spend even a part of your date talking about your ex-lover, spouse or ex anything. You'll lose either way. If you tell him the ex was wonderful, he spends his time trying to figure out what's wrong with *you* and why you're not still together. If the ex was a yutz, he'll assume you were a bigger yutz for picking him. And if he was abusive, it's simply better left unsaid. There will be plenty of time once you have developed a true sense of intimacy to confide and share it with him. If he asks, just say, "When we know each other a little better." This not only gets you off the hook, it also creates that air of mystery that's powerfully enticing without being dishonest.

Rule #4 - Don't Try To Look Like "Dixie In Distress"

We used to believe that if we created the illusion of being tied to the railroad tracks, some handsome Mountie would ride along and rescue us. If you believe this, chances are you'll get flattened like a pancake if you haven't already. It looked so easy when Lucy did it. Ricky would come home and find Lucy pinned against the wall, a nine foot loaf of bread from the oven spearing her in place. "Oh, *Ricky!*" she would wail. And Ricky would make everything all right. The only problem with this train of thought is that if you do indeed find some schmo who enjoys rescuing you, he'll eventually lose interest and get back on his horse as soon as he realizes you're not so helpless after all. Like the first time you tell him to hang a left not a right or he'll miss the exit.

Rule #5 - Quit Touching So Much

Todd, a great looking twenty-five year old fitness trainer, who was one of my first interviews years ago, told me something back then that I have heard again and again since from literally hundreds of men. And each time I relay it to women, I see faces that flicker with a mixture of horror and relief.

"I met a great girl at a party, she was attractive, fun, and we had a lot in common, but she kept touching me. At first I thought she was just showing friendship, but as the night wore on, it began to get on my nerves. When I walked her to her car, she took my arm when we crossed the street, which was fine. But when we went back to her apartment and started talking again, she'd grope my arm, touch my knee or tap me on the shoulder every time she made a point in conversation. She made me feel weird." When I pressed him further, he almost couldn't explain why, but it was clear that it made him physically and emotionally uncomfortable. "I thought she was getting *way* too familiar too soon."

Body language and touch is an important tool for communicating and creating intimacy with someone. However, too much of a good thing too soon is disastrous. Men feel instantly comfortable with someone who will extend a hand (the bonding handshake that is familiar to them, for example) but caresses are different. Women who emphasize a point *selectively* with a touch, show men interest and attention, and men absolutely love that. It simply has to be done with restraint, at the right times and properly, otherwise you'll be unwittingly giving the signal you're clingy and needy. Especially on the first date, don't grope to take his hand, let him find yours. Don't reach for his arm when walking, let him offer it. Don't smooth his tie, or push away a wisp of hair, or wipe away the broccoli adhered to his top lip. Of course, don't be a tin soldier, just remember... a little dab will do ya.

RULE #6 - WATCH WHAT YOU WEAR

"I first met Bonnie at a company softball game. I knocked her down trying to tag her out at second base," said Bill, a twenty-nine year old advertising account rep. "We had instant chemistry. We went out for pizza and beer afterward and really seemed to hit it off. I called her a few days later and made plans to go to dinner and a movie the following Saturday. When I got to the door I couldn't believe it was the same girl. She had on a see-through net top with a black bra underneath, jeans and boots that screamed *Screw me!* at least to me. I was sort of shocked. I hardly knew her. I know I shouldn't judge a book by its cover, but I'm just not attracted to someone who'd be that provocative on the first date."

An interesting point is that Bonnie isn't that way *at all*. But some women think that every man thinks with his groin, subscribing to the antiquated notion that if you look like a molten ball of fire, he'll go wild with desire.

At a singles' night arranged by a large bookstore chain, I spoke to a rather eclectic group of men and women and then opened the floor to questions. About midway through, a woman of about thirty, dressed in an off-the-shoulder white lace blouse, a biker leather vest, skin-tight jeans, and high-heeled granny boots stood up. She was physically stunning with a great face and body. She earnestly asked me why it was she was meeting the kind of men who only wanted one thing and one thing only. During a very long, dead pause in which I'm sure the entire room expected me to say something cryptic; I decided to call a spade a spade. I asked her to tell me what she'd call someone with a white satin dress and a veil. "A bride," she said. And what would you call a man who came in here in a blue uniform and a badge? "A cop," she said. By then I knew she got it and I didn't want to embarrass her. She really did seem like a very nice girl. So I said, "You're obviously a beautiful woman, and if you go to any lengths to accentuate that, people are stuck judging books by their covers. Wear what makes you happy and what makes you feel good; just understand the signal it may be sending."

Also, remember that's true in reverse. If you're only wearing sensible pumps and dresses that come to your knees, the fastest thing you can do to spice up your life is hit the seamstress and shop for shoes on the wild side. Somewhere between space shoes and heels that will give you a nose bleed is a look that will get a man's attention without giving them him wrong idea. Hundreds of men have confided a general rule of thumb: tastefully sexy is a turn-on. Overt and provocative, while being a powerful surprise once the relationship has blossomed, is a true turn-off on a first date.

Rule #7: No Sex

I know I sound like the world's biggest prude, but even if your temperature would burst your home thermometer and you'd like to tear his clothes off with your teeth, Don't! It's way too soon. You don't know what his agenda is or if he is compatible on anything other than a physical level. *Please, please* don't think by giving him the night of his life he'll be on your front porch tomorrow begging for more. Sometimes it works in reverse. Most men have explained that they really don't expect it or necessarily want it.

"It's exciting when you just meet someone and are so turned on by them to want to take them straight to bed," says Ted, a forty-two year old magazine art director. "But when I'm halted, certainly in the beginning, I can't stop thinking about them and when *it's* going to happen. When it happens too soon the mystery and excitement dissipates too fast."

Rule #8: If Dining In a Restaurant: Don't Order Anything That Can't Be Inconspicuously Removed From Your Chest Without Leaving A Whopping Stain Confirming Its Presence In The First Place

Whether or not you realize it, Murphy and his cronies will always be present on first dates. Just for laughs, if nothing else. As wonderful as those olives and chick peas in cream sauce may taste, if there's a chance you can't spear it and get it to your face without it falling through or off your fork... don't order it. Period. No matter how well the rest of the date goes, if a huge chunk of red sauce is staring up at you from your right breast, you'll be so self-conscious you won't be able to enjoy anything further.

There are lots of rules for first date conduct in a restaurant.

Here are three:

Don't eat off his plate once you've vacuumed yours clean.

Don't guzzle so much wine that you ask the piano player if you can sit alongside him and play chopsticks as a duet.

Don't order so much food that he has to leave his car keys as collateral.

The rest of the stuff is common sense or you can ask Leticia Baldridge.

Chapter 11

Dating Do's & Dating Dont's -
A Practical Guide

There are plenty of innovative ways to tackle the on-going I-need-a-date-dilemma. Bill Machmer and three of his buddies from Houston, Texas each paid $2,500 and advertised for love on a billboard: *Four middle class white males 32-39 seek wives.* It's short, snappy and a sure-fire attention getter. Within weeks over 1,000 letters arrived and they found themselves on "Donahue" and in *People* magazine. The problem is, most of us are not that overt. This chapter provides sure-fire tips for improving your odds of getting a date and then dating smart. But no relationship book can give a foolproof guarantee that what you do will always meet with success. Men are different, situations are different and thousands of variables enter into play, including hidden agendas. As sympathetic as I am to the millions of very decent, honorable men who are out there seeking the same things we are, I'm cognizant that there is a periphery of them who's sole aim in life is to cause us pain and misery. And that's another whole topic (see Chapter 18). However, what this chapter does, is address the things the majority of men absolutely love and the things that make them run for cover:

DATING DO'S AND DON'TS:
DON'T BOX YOURSELF IN BY BEING SO RIGID

"I won't, I absolutely will not ever call a man," said Janey.
"Why?" I asked gently, seeing she was getting visibly upset.
"It's just not right. If he's interested let him call me."

Calling a man has always been a touchy subject with some women. And lest I bring the fury of all women upon me, let me say it has a lot to do with age. If you were a teenager prior to the '60s you grew up believing nice girls didn't do that, hence you tried to bring your daughter up to believe that, too. Some abided, some didn't. And, as some women became more bold in the workplace, some did so in their personal lives. Some men loved it, some were appalled. That's what makes horse races. During the '60s through the '80s, we began to hear horror stories about guerrilla women and their dating tactics. "If you're standing in a doorway and see a great guy coming your way, stick your foot out. He'll fall and break his tibia in front of you and you can give him your number on the way to emergency. Or crash your cart into him at the supermarket while he's groping for grapes. This way, as you're apologizing, you can ask him to dinner tomorrow." Anything and everything became fair game. While necessity is the mother of invention, some women got drunk on the power and control it gave them, and men started talking about **aggressive** women. Then they started to duck them.

Just when the rest of us slowpokes were bravely reaching for the phone, we get our hands slapped by the broadness of the aggressive label. I hope, if nothing else, the '90s is documented as the decade where the dust finally settled; where the excesses, (drugs, alcohol, material possessions and behavior included) went completely out of vogue and priorities came back into focus.

There is a cavernous difference between picking up the phone and telling a man you have an extra Knicks' ticket, and hitting him on the head with a club before dragging him off by the hair to your cave. "I love it when a woman I'm interested in invites me out. And she doesn't have to spend money on me either," offered Ralph, a thirty-three year old veterinarian. "Even over to her place for a meal, a picnic or brunch or a bowl of soup and a movie. It just shows me she's not taking advantage of me and that she's interested. What I shy away from is a gal I'm not sure I'm interested in, sending me cutesy cards, leaving cryptic messages on my machine, feigning chance meetings and constantly calling me in the hopes of sparking more interest. That's a turn off. I still want to do the pursuing, especially while I'm deciding how deep my interest is."

Most men adore it when a woman takes the initiative. It takes some of the fear of rejection off them. It shows interest. It shows confidence. But it's like anything else. It's all in how you do it. Handing a man you meet in a seminar your business card saying, "I thought you brought up some good points. I'd be interested in meeting you if you're not already involved," is a great way to break the ice. You've got nothing to lose. You've stated interest and why, *and you've given him an out.* If he's not interested he can say he's involved, but if he's not, you could be having dinner. And what's the big deal about rejection? Your friends will still love you, you'll still have your job and Spot, your pet Mastiff will still greet you at the door with a sloppy, wet one. People risk rejection daily in their jobs, but in their personal lives they hide under rocks.

If you want to start enjoying life, attract the kind of man who'll be your prince. So what if you have to hand twelve toads a business card first? Some men might rebuff you, perceiving aggression, some because of their own insecurity and some because they're just jerks who wouldn't know a pearl if the oyster flew up and hit them between the eyes. But who cares? If you do it with grace enough times, there will be a great guy (or many) who will simply be intrigued and flattered. Learning how to successfully play the dating game means being a little less rigid. Giving up the way you used to do things, acquainting yourself with new concepts and remembering not to be too hard on yourself when at first it doesn't work. You wouldn't yell at your child when she fell off her bicycle after just removing her training wheels. Take another deep breath and picture yourself bumping into a neat guy, initiating a short conversation and saying, "I'm a little awkward at this, but you seem to be a nice guy, if you're not already involved with someone, I'd love to meet for coffee or a drink. Here's my card." It sure as hell beats sitting at home with the Mastiff and Ben and Jerry.

Finding a man who's right for you means taking control of your life and putting some effort into it. Picking up the phone to call a man won't earmark you for the Scarlet Letter; putting his number in speed dial *will*.

Do Network

I know. Everyone tells you that. Networking successfully means a lot of work. It's usually well worth the effort, but half of us have our hands full just keeping what's on our already full plate from overflowing. Networking means just that. Joining organizations, working on committees and attending functions where you can meet men, right? Half right. Most of us think that you have to put yourself where the men are and that indeed is very important. What we overlook is meeting other great women who have single fathers, uncles, brothers or sexy co-workers. Extending your female circle of acquaintances can be unbelievably rewarding. Most single women will introduce you to their rejects which is not as horrific as it sounds. One woman's trash is another's treasure, since we all have different agendas. But moms, sisters and best-buddies might know someone perfect for you. If you have the time, it's an alternate avenue that has tremendous promise and you also get to befriend some great women. If you don't have the time, you can always do what my friend Suzanne does with more aplomb than anyone I know. She gives a party and invites any great eligible man she's met that she's interested in. Being in public relations, she has access to hordes of eligible men. She frequently plans little cocktail parties or Sunday brunches and invites some couples, some women she doesn't consider too threatening, and her objects of interest by saying, "I'm having a few friends in for a little get together; It's a great group of people and I'd love you to come if you don't have previous plans." They get a glimpse of the sweet, at-home Suzanne and she has the opportunity to meet and chat close-up with no uncomfortable pressure.

If you're an organizer, there are a great many wonderful ideas like coordinating a "pot luck" cocktail party or buffet. You supply the house, paper goods and fixin's (as much or as little as you care to contribute) and each of your guests brings an item. These are great fun; you coordinate the guest list and now have a great way to break the ice with single men, single and others you've wanted to get to know more intimately. You can also do these where every guest you invite must bring one single person of the opposite sex. This way you'll have a constant supply of new social contacts. The bonus is you'll also give these ideas to other people and be invited to their get-togethers. A little effort goes a long way.

Another networking technique that works is to flatter someone who deals with the public who you genuinely like—the butcher, the grocer, or the pharmacist, even if he's married. "You're such a wonderful guy, if only you had a brother." Maybe he does, or maybe he'll file it and next time Mr. Wonderful comes in for toothpaste or pork chops, he'll say, "There's this great lady that comes in here, I think you'd love meeting her." It works with women, too.

DON'T LOOK DOWN

Instead of walking with your head down, go slower, keep your head up and smile. Make eye contact. When you feel good, and are hopeful, the possibilities are endless.

When you do date, it's important to know what kinds of things turn men off the most. From a survey of almost 700 men, here is the list that made the top ten:

Don't be habitually late

Moms counseled us to be fashionably late. A few minutes is fine or if there's an unavoidable circumstance. But don't think this is how to be alluring. Habitual lateness is blatant disrespect for the person you keep waiting.

Don't keep taking the emotional temperature of the relationship

Men hate that kind of constant probing and equate it with nagging or being in a choke-hold. Accept that things are going fine, unless there are specific signs they aren't, then bring it up for discussion. Don't keep asking him for constant emotional assurance. A daily State of the Relationship Address is not only a royal pain in the butt for most men, but they start to associate the discomfort it creates *with being around you*. The end result: you're doing it to gain a comfort level, but in the process you're making him uncomfortable.

Don't keep taking his emotional temperature

"Women just don't realize how much this turns men off," said Marshall, a thirty-seven year old horse-trainer from Kentucky.

As women, we're such intuitional creatures, many times avoiding storms because our little voice warns us in time. However, it goes into overdrive when we're involved in a relationship, so we look for any and every indication of cloudy weather up ahead. "What's the matter? Is something bothering you?" "What's wrong? How come you're in a bad mood?" "Why do you have that look on your face?" "Probing, probing, probing," says Marshall, "gets me angry, puts me in a bad mood and makes me want to get the hell out of there."

If you ask one of these questions and he says "Nothing's wrong." Let it go at that. When he's ready, he'll tell you if it is really "something." The constant probing, which men see as nagging more times than not, drives them further into their funk.

With men as with women, there is not always a comprehendible reason for a "mood." Men tend to look outside themselves for how they feel. Their team wins, they're elated. The boss was angry, he's in a crummy mood. If the mood has nothing to do with you, be kind but ignore it. But rest assured, if you don't, the constant questioning can *create* a bad mood.

Don't make everything right

Women are brought up to nurture and fix things, but doing it constantly while dating is lethal. Not only will most men start to feel mothered and rebel against you as they did with their own moms, but you'll end up resenting having to do everything.

Don't try and woo him by making him jealous

In my surveys of men, it is clear that this is a universal and complete turn off. "I hate game players," said Craig, a forty-one year old Las Vegas pit boss. "It's what I do for a living. I hate it in my personal life. I don't play silly mind games with women and I won't tolerate them being played on me. A lot of women believe men are oblivious to the ploys. We're not." While men have little or no patience for Donna the Doormat, they possess far less for Vivian the Vixen. What was startling to me is that most men *know when we're doing it* and therefore it doesn't work or they back off thinking exactly what Craig does—that you're a game player. Leaving a pair of your father's trousers on the back of your bathroom door, or his shirt in your closet, or sending yourself cards and flowers is rather transparent. The feelings stirred by jealousy should never be confused with desire. Many women mistakenly think that if a man is jealous, it proves he cares. *Wrong*. Men are *naturally* competitive. They may instinctively want to win the contest. You, as the prize, is purely incidental. The only way to make him desire you is to have a full, rich life, lots of outside (him) interests, the self-respect not to turn into Doris the Drivel once you become involved and the confidence to believe you're worth it.

Don't be dishonest

Men will not marry a woman they cannot trust.

Don't think that because you're dating he can't maintain some privacy

"I hate it when a woman I like and have been seeing a while, suddenly starts asking me all kinds of questions. When will you be home? Where are you going after work? When I start seeing someone, I still want to maintain some privacy. I hate when a woman comes over and starts looking for signs of other women right away. Women cross over that privacy line so quickly."

Don't Push

"Women are always reading too much into things too soon. When I say I like her or enjoy being with her, I do. I really mean it. She reads it like I like her only, I enjoy being with her only. And then I start to feel pressure. I may have wanted to go further, but when they start pushing for more, I run the other way, even if I hadn't planned on it. It makes me feel caged."

No matter what we say about the modern man, he still, in most cases, likes to do the pursuing; it's exciting to him.

Don't Hint

"There's nothing that drives me crazier than when the woman I'm dating hints at things. Instead of coming right out and saying that something is bothering her, or asking for what she wants," says Ted, a thirty-one year old mortgage broker from Des Moines, Iowa, "she drops these little clues hoping I'll get it. Then, if I don't pick up on them or have trouble decoding what they mean, she gets sullen or quiet until we end up in this big discussion about how I'm insensitive to her feelings. I'm not insensitive; I'm always willing to talk, but women think they should coyly plant the idea, then we'll bring up the subject. Men don't work that way."

Ted's right. Men *don't* work that way. Throughout this book I write about a women's ability to finely tune her intuition almost to the point of ESP. The little detectors our intuition has working overtime, are always picking up on clues, putting two and two together and decoding innuendo, until we make what we deem to be an educated guess. Men aren't built like that. They take concrete information, process it, and arrive at an answer. They don't do all the fancy footwork along the way. The dilemma is that since the fancy footwork is second nature to us, we expect it to be that way for the guy we're involved with. So we assume he's purposely ignoring us or avoiding issues, when he's *relatively* oblivious. Sure, your mood or the clues you're leaving, tell him something's different, he's just not sure what it means. "It's like I've got that little robot who flailed his arms in the '60s TV show "Lost in Space" screaming, 'Warning! Warning!' in my head. The only thing dropping hints does," said Ira, twenty-eight year old stock room manager from Lima, Ohio, "is get me confused and then angry. Women don't want to say what's on their minds, they want us to guess. Well, I don't want to guess and when I realize that something is not right and that she is dropping hints, I'll ignore it until she tells me. I won't play that stupid guessing game." When you do this during the dating process the other signal you're sending is: "Warning! Warning! If she's like this *now*, what can you expect from her after you say, 'I do'?" *That* little voice he'll listen to. By and large, remember, most men will respect and appreciate a woman who says, "Something is bothering me; would you sit down and discuss it?"

Part Four

How To Marry A Man –
Secrets For Moving The Relationship Up
To The Next Level

Chapter 12

The "Why Factor"
And How To Apply It In Your Own Relationships

Charles F. Kettering once said, "There is a great difference between knowing and understanding. You can know a great deal about something and not really understand it."

Those words are no more apropos then when applied to man-woman relationships. In my life, I have never felt more vulnerable than during those times when something happened to me for which there was no explanation.

In my second or third year of high school, as a normal school day was coming to a close, I heard rumblings about a girl who supposedly was going to 'beat me up', as the phrase goes. I paid no attention for several reasons: first, I had never, ever been involved in anything remotely connected to a fight, and second, because I was the kind of kid who kept to herself, never irritating anyone enough, or so I thought, to cause such a reaction.

As I began to walk the mile or so home from school, suddenly this bully of a girl, with industrial strength mascara, thick black eyeliner and long stringy hair, appeared out of nowhere and started taunting me about *taking* her boyfriend. I had no idea who she was or what she was talking about. Perhaps she had mistaken me for someone else? As I started to look around, my mind started to race a mile a minute and my heart started to pound as every person's would knowing something bad is about to happen. I'll spare you the details, but *she* had a fight, I just happened to be the object she chose to have it with. What did I know about fighting? It was like a surreal scene from a Fellini movie.

It wasn't until about a week later, as the ostrich egg-sized bulge on the back of my noggin was starting to deflate, that I learned who she was and the whole reason she instigated the fight... she liked a boy she *heard* liked me. *I hadn't even heard he liked me!* When he did indeed ask me to go steady about three weeks later, I almost blackened *his* eye. I didn't cause, perpetuate or even deserve what had happened to me and nothing I could have done in this situation would have altered the outcome. Perhaps I could have reasoned with her, "Excuse me Attila, before you bludgeon me into guacamole dip, might you consider the fact that perhaps you have the wrong person?" I don't think that would have changed the situation, but finally learning what caused her reaction, misguided as it was, did alleviate some of the confusion.

In a roundabout way, this is the identical situation many women find themselves in with the men they date and vice versa.

"We had such a great time together; he said he'd call by Friday and I never heard from him again."

"We talked all night, we had so many common interests, she let me buy her drinks and then she gave me a wrong phone number."

For most of us, not knowing *why* something happened or didn't happen, for that matter, drives us crazy. We analyze the situation until we can't think anymore. When the blank fills in, we can at least comprehend, although we still may not be able to catalyze the outcome—that understanding affords us unique insight into preventing it, preparing for it or avoiding it in the future. And that tool, what I have come to call the "Why Factor", is a powerful ally when establishing lasting bonds with a love partner.

THE "WHY FACTOR" IN PRACTICE

Thirty-four year old Sue Ellen, an associate producer for a

network talk show, told me an interesting story while she kept me company in the greenroom. "I had been seeing Mark for about ten months before we finally decided to move in together, just after Halloween," she began. "I knew I loved him and living together was something I had really wanted, so I was determined to do everything right." Up to this point she had been in several relationships but most of them were just dating relationships that seldom lasted over eight months to a year, and none had been the "permanent live-in" kind where your stuff and his stuff occupy space at the same residence at the same time.

"This was a relationship I was determined to make work," she continued. "Around Thanksgiving time, I decided to make a big family dinner, hopefully to bring us closer together and to make him see that this could be permanent between us. He thought it was a good idea, although now in retrospect, I can't say he jumped for joy as we shopped for the necessary items together. A few days before, he started to get what I can only describe as *distant*. Thanksgiving morning he got up and straightened the apartment but he wouldn't go near the kitchen once anyone arrived. Our families got along really well, but he just wasn't himself the whole day—quiet and moody. I kept asking him what was wrong, and he kept saying 'Nothing.' After everyone left he helped me clean-up, but every time I broached the subject of his mood he became more distant and visibly irritated. Before it intensified into a full-fledged fight, I let up and after a few days it all blew over.

"The weeks before Christmas were great. We shopped, stopped for happy-hours and had a wonderful time at my office party and then at his. Everything was perfect right up until I brought a small Christmas tree home as a surprise. I bought the lights, the garland, the glass ornaments and a bottle of sixty-five dollar champagne, to celebrate our first Christmas together."

"What happened?" I asked.

"It was a disaster," she said. "He barely looked at the tree, he opened the packages of lights but wouldn't really participate. The harder I pushed, the more aggravated he seemed to get, until he said that the champagne was giving him a headache and he went to bed. That was it. I sat there hurt and stunned till 2 am all by myself. I didn't want to fight during the holidays, and the next night, Christmas Eve, we were going to his mom and dad's, so I ignored the whole thing and put aside how hurt I was so we could have a pleasant time at his parents.

"Once we got there it was like a lightening bolt came down from the heavens and struck me. His sister Anne and her husband were there and Anne had the same blank look Mark had. It wasn't until their mom started assigning decorating duties that I even understood *why*. 'Mark,' she said, 'why don't you get Aunt Sylvia's handmade ornaments out of the garage. Anne, you start untangling the lights. Sue Ellen, you unwrap the painted crystal icicles. Pete, Pete, where's Pete,?' she asked with alarm. Pete, Mark's dad had the good sense to feign food poisoning and probably spent the rest of the night rereading *War and Peace* in the upstairs bathroom. He obviously had been through this before.

"I'll save the rest of the gory details, but suffice it to say that the rest of the evening went much like the beginning, except that wherever Mark and Anne placed anything, anywhere, she moved it to someplace she thought was better."

I asked Sue Ellen if she ever talked to Mark about it and the incident. She said no, that he never seemed to want to talk about it. So even though they hadn't discussed it, at least now she wasn't taking his reactions personally; and he seemed happiest forgetting about it for another eleven months.

Sue Ellen is one of the few of Mark's girlfriend's who lasted more than a couple of holiday seasons without leaving him feeling hurt and dejected as Sue Ellen would have, had she not put two-and-two together. Of course, she embellished the mother's behavior a bit, but the reality was that few, if any of the women in Mark's life were ever astute enough to find the root of his behavior. They just reacted to it, not realizing they had done nothing to cause it, and that Mark's reaction wasn't *directed at them*. Many women, and many men for that matter, tend to internalize a situation like this and either quietly suffer the hurt or escalate it until inevitably, the relationship ends.

"Once I understood why Mark acted the way he did, and understood it wasn't caused by something I had or hadn't done, I was able to be compassionate towards him. I actually felt bad for him. Christmas was always such a joyous time in our house. Now in my own way, I'm quietly giving him his space and putting some of the joy of Christmas back in the holiday for him. I don't push and I don't expect. Last year he even picked the tree out with me and volunteered to untangle the lights. We drank wine, listened to Christmas music and although I decorate the tree primarily by myself, he's at least there sharing the moments with me."

Now, about four years later, Mark still adores Sue Ellen and is a wonderful companion in most every other area that's important to her. He's kind, he loves animals as she does, he cooks and willingly shares the household duties, he's funny and loving and is totally monogamous. This is the man of Sue Ellen's dreams, yet in this one particular area, if she hadn't taken the time to *understand why* he acted as he did, it would have started an avalanche of problems in the relationship that ultimately would have caused its demise. By taking the time to unearth the "why" behind Mark's behavior, the relationship continued to flourish and in December of this year (of all months), they'll be married.

While the "Why Factor" (understanding the cause behind the action) is indeed the cornerstone of this book, playing an integral part in most every chapter, it isn't a magic potion or cure-all. However, if you have patience and care enough, it will give you the insight needed to get the relationship to the next level. Too many relationships prematurely disintegrate because the injured party is reactive to the hurt they feel, tending to retaliate rather than become reflective. Hey, we're only human, but in dealing with as many men, women and relationships as I do, I have come to realize that even in the throes of being hurt, when the injured party takes the time to do some detective work rather than simply go on the defensive (which only alleviates the sting momentarily and almost always makes it worse in the long run), they usually end up *saving* the relationship, often times making it stronger.

We've all been too judgmental at times in our lives, especially when we're alienated and our hearts are on the line. But if the man you're dating developed heat bumps every time he ventured out in the sun, you'd have compassion and you'd *understand why* he didn't particularly care to spend his Sundays frying like an egg in Crisco. Some reactions are emotional and not as easy to see as a heat rash might be.

LEARNING TO INVOKE THE WHY FACTOR
STEP 1: THINK, BEFORE YOU REACT

This means making a conscious effort. No matter how stupid the question asked by your co-worker, how many times the waitress forgets your iced tea, or how many times he misplaces your remote control, stop, take a deep breath and calmly try to resolve the situation. You may feel silly at first, because you're used to being quick on the draw, but I promise, if you follow this, it gets easier and suddenly, some of the weight of the world is lifted *off* your back. (The bonus is, the effects are also cumulative.) It doesn't mean, however, that your coworker won't still ask a dumb question or that no waiter will ever again forget your drink; it just means that you personally will be less affected, less likely to sustain those effects further and thus, eliminate the possibility of negative impact.

I remember saying to waitresses impatiently, "I asked for an iced tea about a half hour ago, *remember?*" Sure, she brought it, but now we were both in a huff. Then one day I tried it like this: "I'm sorry, I know you're probably having a really hectic day but you kinda forgot my iced tea again." I got ten *I'm sorry's* and at the end of the meal, just before she brought my check, she brought me a cookie, and in whipped cream had made a happy face. It may not seem like much, but it meant a lot. Her day wasn't made worse, I didn't go back to work all bent out of shape. In fact, the cookie put me in such a good mood that I seemed nicer to the other people around me and they responded by being nicer to me.

Remember, attracting the kind of love partner you want, is not a quick fix. You can't pop a pill. It's a lifestyle change, the same basic principle as any sensible diet.

STEP 2: GIVE THE BENEFIT OF THE DOUBT

In the hurry up, survival-of-the-fittest world we live in, this is no easy task. What I've learned however, is that as I get older, it becomes less and less important to be right; it's far more important to be fair. By giving the benefit of the doubt, I certainly am not suggesting you turn yourself into Silly Putty. Just that before you write off, blow up at or discount someone in your life, you make sure you understand their motives and are not just jumping to a conclusion, however likely the conclusion may seem.

"I met her on Friday night and the following Friday we went to dinner and walked and talked for twenty blocks while window shopping," said a twenty-nine year old ad agency creative director from Atlanta. "I didn't want to seem too anxious, so I decided to wait until Monday or Tuesday to call and ask her out again. Monday at noon my boss comes into my office with two plane tickets and tells me to go home and pack because we were leaving for Chicago at five. It was an audience with a client, the agency had being trying to land forever. I rushed home, did some laundry, packed, got my files together and left. When I got home Wednesday, I was swamped with work. It wasn't until the following Sunday that I saw her number on my cork board. 'Oh my God,' I thought and picked up the phone to explain. From her first hello, she was cold and distant. Not at all like the girl I laughed a whole night with. I realized she must be upset and tried to explain the unusual set of circumstances. In one of the most accusatory voices I had ever heard, except when I was seven and broke my mother's favorite candy dish, she said, 'It's a shame all ten of your fingers were broken at the same time.' I didn't know what to say. I had really just met her but thought this is a girl I could see myself getting into a serious relationship with. I really believed I could care for this girl. Sure I was remiss in not phoning sooner but it wasn't like there was any implied commitment. I was more than willing to make amends and explain. She didn't even give me the benefit of the doubt."

This gal wrote him off as uninterested and whether she was reacting from hurt or anger, she slammed the door shut.

The same kind of situation ended up very differently when Jack, a great-looking forty-nine year old highway patrolman from Texas who was widowed, told it. During his *Bachelor Book* magazine interview, we asked him what he was looking for in a partner. "A woman, just like my late wife." came the instantaneous reply.

"What made your wife so special?" we quizzed.

"From the time we met, she just made me feel good about myself, even when I did the dumbest things. After our first date, I took what I thought was her number and put it under my phone so I wouldn't misplace it. I went to call her two days later and what I thought was her number was a note to myself telling me to buy Comet and paper towels! That meant the number was still in my blue jeans, which meant, oh God, they were now in the washer. I ran down to the laundry room, pulled out the jeans and the number wasn't there. It turned up about five days later, at the bottom of the hamper—the one place I hadn't looked. I was almost afraid to call, afraid she would have thought I wasn't interested, or worse, maybe that she wasn't interested anymore. When I said, 'Hi, this is Jack,' she said, 'Jack, Jack, Jack, let me see... tall, good looking, absent-minded cop.' Then she said, 'It's a good thing I didn't hold my breath.' Never once did she make me feel silly, or awkward or *beholding*. When I told her what happened she just laughed."

A man falls in love with a woman because of the way he feels about himself when he's with her. Men who stray, ironically provide tremendous insight into this. "My ex-wife said my cheating on her was the reason our marriage broke up. It wasn't," confided Alex, a fifty-two year old menswear executive. "I was never the kind of man who'd even think of having an affair. Being monogamous was a commitment I made when we married. But our relationship died. It came to a screeching halt and we existed as two separate people who lived in the same house. Then I started working with a woman designer at our company. She's forty-eight with three teenagers and she isn't overly fit, if you know what I mean. But to me, she's beautiful. She laughed at my jokes. She doesn't turn every conversation into a contest of wills and she genuinely likes me. I feel smart with her. I feel attractive when I'm with her. I don't have to fight to prove everything I say. She values my opinion. She's not clingy, or needy. I feel in-love when I'm with her. I can't remember when someone made me feel so good about myself. Then again maybe I do. It was about twenty-eight years ago... when I married my ex-wife. Our relationship was over for years, it's just that neither of us had the courage to acknowledge it or walk away. My ex-wife thinks I cheated on her. I think spending twenty years in a marriage that's dead is cheating on yourself."

STEP 3: PUT YOURSELF IN THE OTHER PERSON'S SHOES

To paraphrase a native American proverb, you can't understand a man until you've walked a mile in his moccasins. Taken as a caution, Step 3 can be used to uncover an answer for almost any given reaction, thereby providing insight into where things have gotten turned upside down and how to counteract it, not merely judge and react to it. It is this information and how to successfully find and use it, that is necessary to develop trust, and *trust is the one element that promotes intimacy the quickest.*

As mothers, we do this all the time with babies. If a child is crying we search to discover why. We may change the diaper if the baby is wet. Sometimes that solves the problem. Sometimes it doesn't. We'll give them a bottle. Sometimes that fixes it.

This is the most basic of human relationships and we can and should glean something from it. Mothers provide the majority of the needs a baby has after birth, the baby feels safe and loved and trusts the mother. When the baby gets hurt, who's the first person he calls for? *Mommy*. By putting yourself in the other person's shoes and not reacting negatively right away, you have the opportunity to see the situation clearly. Yet scant few take the time to do that within our male/female relationships, and fewer know how to do it successfully without escalating the problem.

"I remember the day I knew I wanted to marry my wife," said Travis, a forty-two year old bank executive. "We were driving to her sister's wedding from New Jersey to Connecticut. It was the first time I was meeting her whole family together. I was a wreck, but I was trying to look cool. I missed not one exit but two. I finally got so lost trying to get us back to the first exit, I had to stop and ask directions. When I pulled into the gas station, instead of telling me what a yutz I was, Peggy said, 'Someday we'll have to come back here and visit, it's so quaint.' She had every opportunity to go for my jugular but she didn't. She didn't make me feel stupid, she didn't point out that I screwed up and she didn't attack me. At that moment I had such love for her, I knew she was someone I wanted to be with."

The "Why Factor" is a tool, that if used correctly, affords one clarity to explore then examine what makes men feel threatened, weak, confused and how that *causes* them to react. The above situation could have turned into a disaster with *both* people arriving at the party hurt, angry and upset. Peggy was mature enough to realize that Travis knew he screwed up, reasoning that he was nervous too. She knew he didn't mean to get them lost and she didn't exacerbate the situation by pointing it out. Instead, she handled it by keeping her cool and allowing him to keep his dignity. She didn't make him feel as if he were less of a man.

It is because most women and men do not understand *what*

inaugurates certain reactions in each other and *why* and *from where* they stem, that has caused much of the damage done within relationships, damage that could have been avoided. The old adage, "the first cut is the deepest," has significant meaning when applied to solidifying a lasting bond.

When queried about what they look for in a woman, clearly over 85% of the men responded by saying, "A woman who knows how to make me feel good about myself." As women, we're finely-tuned, intuitive machines that sometimes know the answer before the question is asked. Men, on the other hand, with some very rare exceptions, aren't as finely-tuned. Many times we have the luxury of catching ourselves before we make the mistake. Often times men will make the mistake and then repair the damage.

In love relationships, or even in friendships, it's not always necessary to have the last word, especially if that word affirms the blame. It takes a split second to shatter someone's self-esteem and confidence, and it may take two to think of a way to build it up. Most people know when they've goofed, pointing it out only compounds it. Peggy's reaction made Travis feel safe, and he exploded with love for her. A caustic remark at that moment would only have caused him to fire a shot back at her to maintain his self-esteem, leaving both partners angry and upset. Peggy is one of those lucky women who instinctively knew how to build and instill trust.

Women need to understand that most men are indeed extremely emotional, they're just not comfortable expressing it. But discomfort expressing emotion doesn't indicate they don't *feel* hurt, frightened, confused and overwhelmed, the same way we do. Developing your own ability to invoke the "Why Factor" in your personal relationships may take time. "It's harder than it looks, but then Rome wasn't built in a day.

The "Why Factor" may be deemed a somewhat spiritual exercise, for it sets you up to treat others as you would be treated yourself—wisdom that comes from a book far more enduring than this one. When you are successful in relationships, you optimize the potential for wonderful people, wonderful opportunities and a wonderful life partner to enter your world.

Chapter 13 | Determining Lifestyle Compatibility

If there's one question I'm asked most often it's got to be: "What's the biggest mistake singles make?" I don't think there are any hard-and-fast answers when it comes to emotions and relationships. However, having said that, there is one pitfall I see which dooms many a relationship. The paradox is, it's one of the simplest things to overcome, but the most difficult to identify. It's called *expectation*. It's defined by Webster's New World Dictionary as: looking forward to; anticipation of or *looking towards something as if it is due*. That last definition is the one that puts our modern day relationships at risk. Prior to an intimacy, many of us never develop a clear picture of just what we expect out of our lives or our partners, beyond "I'd like him to be handsome and rich and have only one flaw—an allergy to Kryptonite." Or, "I want her to look like Christie Brinkley, make love like Jessica Hahn and balance a checkbook like Hillary Clinton." Beyond some superficial things, most of us don't devote any time to really thinking about *lifestyle compatibility*. We always assume we'll know it when we see it. If only it would be that simple.

"Everyone saw it coming but Mary," said the sister-in-law of a rather distraught forty year old Canadian beauty. "We could see Michael loved her, but she was squeezing the life out of him. I didn't ever think Mary did anything to purposely hurt or infuriate him. She genuinely did everything out of love, but after seven years of marriage Michael wouldn't even answer a question unless he first looked in her direction for approval. In a restaurant with three other couples, after he placed his order for a medium steak and a baked potato, Mary chastised him about his cholesterol. 'Wouldn't the broiled chicken and a salad be better for you?' she said. He changed his order.

I tracked Michael down for an interview because I thought his answers might have some value for thousands of women who find themselves in similar situations, loving a man, but also struggling to mold him into her vision. When I found him, he was happily living in Georgia with a southern belle named Emily.

"It's been two years since the divorce and I feel like a new man," he offered enthusiastically. "Don't get me wrong, it's not that Mary was an ogre; she was the perfect wife—attractive, petite. She kept herself in shape, gave great dinner parties, always dressed beautifully in the latest fashion. She came from a good family. She had class but she created this upwardly mobile, perfectly trendy lifestyle for us, only she forgot to ask me if I wanted it. Everything was for show—the fabulous house in the right neighborhood, the right caterer for the parties. We had to belong to the "in" gym rather than the one that was closest to our house. We were the "perfect" couple, only as each day went by, I remembered less and less of why we fell in love. We couldn't go away for a spur-of-the-moment weekend because so and so's party was scheduled at the same time. I wouldn't go out with the guys from work because she didn't get along with their wives. I was dying to go bowling and she admitted she wouldn't be caught dead in a bowling alley. I thought the truth was because she didn't want to risk her manicure. I got to the point where I didn't think I had a vote or say in *anything*. I was just following this predetermined path. If I did get fed up and confront her, she'd either ignore me for a week, as if I was dead, or moan and nag until I came around. I'm only forty-four, I just couldn't imagine living the next twenty years like that.

"Maybe it was partly my fault," he continued. "In the beginning, I did want to make her happy and I really didn't have a whole lot of preferences. It didn't matter to me if we saw one movie over the other, and it was nice to have a woman who wasn't afraid to make a decision. I just don't know how I got from not caring what movie I saw, to having *her* decide what food I wanted to order in a restaurant."

Completely devastated by the divorce, Mary initially thought Michael would come back, so she sat by and waited, and waited and waited. She waited so long, that she was forced to sell the house and many of the possessions which meant so much to her. She ended up living with family for over a year until the reality of her situation sunk in. For someone like Mary, to whom perceptions were everything, this was a devastating blow to her psyche that she still has not fully recovered from. She had her entire self-worth caught up in how her life was *perceived* by the world. A long sabbatical out east with another sibling gave her some time to heal and adjust to the reality of her new life. When she returned to Vancouver, it was with an attitude of acceptance. She took a small apartment, bought a less than luxurious car and got her first job in fifteen years.

"Now I know that many of the expectations I had for myself and the kind of life I wanted, I forced onto Michael. I just didn't think that was bad, wanting a nice house and all the accouterments. I thought that's what you were supposed to do, get married, get ahead. That's what my parents did."

"Were your parents happy?," I asked.

After a long pause she said, "My father left when I was sixteen. I hadn't really thought about it before."

Mary genuinely loved Michael, and in her own way was only doing what she thought was best for him, and what unconsciously she thought would bond him to her forever. If she were the perfect wife and the perfect hostess, if they had the most beautiful house and the snazziest car, if they ascended the social ladder *together*, then he wouldn't leave her. She just forgot to stop and ask him if that's what *he* wanted too, and inadvertently caused their marriage to come apart at the seams.

"I don't know exactly how I got where I am," said a striking forty-five year old former retailer. "All I know is that I've spent the last fourteen years pursuing my husband's dream, and I knew I couldn't do it anymore. When we married we were very much in love, we had hopes and dreams like everyone else. We worked hard, got a nice house, nice cars, two kids. Then he wanted a bigger house, so I took a second job and he started a custom jogging suit business on the side. His business grew and grew and he needed more help, so he pushed me to quit my job. I did. We were working nights and weekends and as the business expanded, I was the traffic controller, the bookkeeper, the head of production—things I didn't want to do. As time went on I tried to tell him that this wasn't for me, that I wasn't happy. I wanted us to have a life. He accused me of having no drive, no desire to get ahead and sabotaging our dreams. But I was happy with the house and car I already had. I didn't need a Mercedes and I didn't think the kids had to be in designer jeans; I wanted the free time to enjoy my life. He was always trying to make the business bigger, getting the clothes in more outlets, more, more, more. We didn't have a life together anymore. We couldn't even talk without arguing. I guess I kept going with it because I kept hoping that if we just did this, we'd have time to ourselves. If we just did that, we'd finally get to the pinnacle that would make him happy and then we could stop and smell the roses. I don't think there is anything wrong with him wanting to be a mogul, but I didn't want to be a mogul too.

"When he started pushing my daughter into tennis and piano lessons and my son to play baseball and football, I confronted him. 'I just want my kids to have everything I didn't,' he said. 'I don't want them to feel like I did growing up, like I was always on the outside looking in. My family barely had the money to dress and feed us. There never was anything left for anything extra.'

He thought I was nuts to just let them pick and choose

what they wanted to do. But when I was a kid if my brother and I wanted to join a club or learn a craft we just asked and my parents enrolled us. When we developed an interest in something else, they just enrolled us in something else. We came from such different backgrounds, I just never thought these things could become such issues."

MISCONCEPTION #1: BELIEVING THAT DIFFERENT BACKGROUNDS AND DIFFERENT GOALS WON'T MATTER

Once we become more intimate, we project our hopes, our dreams and expectations on our partners. And if that isn't difficult enough, we're often products of vastly different lifestyles, each carrying into the relationship our own emotional baggage and perhaps even the expectations held by our parents.

Suddenly, we have an image of the perfect life and the perfect relationship. An image extending to who our partner should be, how he or she should act and think. Some even take it to extremes, setting goals and limits for their partners. How he should speak, what he should wear and what foods he should eat. But sometimes the first fatal blow we deal our relationships is forgetting to keep discussing, asking and discerning whether or not the person we've chosen to become involved with is of like mind. Make no mistake, helping to improve a partner is an integral part of loving them. Wanting your partner to be the best they can be is admirable; trying to *change the person they are* is disastrous. Lovers are not like houses. The fixer-upper is a good deal on the real estate market, but lethal in love.

Chapter 14
Monkey See, Monkey Do - How Our Parents' Relationships Impact Our Own

"Oh my God," yelled an attractive twenty-nine year old make-up artist from Arizona. "I'm turning into my mother. I just told my new boyfriend to make sure he took an umbrella because it looked like rain today."

There are few among us who haven't caught ourselves in horror as we spew words that seem to come from our mothers' mouths, not ours. And I'm not *mommy-bashing* as my mom likes to call it. I love my mom, she's my best friend, it's just that there were things she did, I swore I'd never do or say when I grew up. And when I least expect it, my head whirls around like Linda Blair's in *The Exorcist* and out pops my mom's voice from between my Revlon sienna colored lips, "You tell the lawn guy that he forgot to weed whack under the orange tree and he never edged the patio and..."

"Would you like to speak with the lawn guy yourself?" my husband asks a tad on the sarcastic side?"

My mom was great for always telling my dad what to tell other people, but she wouldn't tell them herself. I swore I'd never do that; so why does this happen when we consciously will ourselves *not* to do it?

Because we are partly creatures of our environment.

"I was cut to the quick," explained Steve, a forty-four year old divorced father from San Antonio, Texas as he explained the turmoil in his marriage, "when my wife asked for a divorce,

I went through the motions like an alien. I thought everything was fine. I went to work, she cared for the house and we had two kids. I didn't realize that I was recreating the patterns of my mom and dad's marriage and living them. My dad would be watching TV and casually ask my mom: 'Do you know what I could go for?' And whatever it was, my mom would be off getting it for him like a rocket. My dad got up after dinner and read the paper, and mom always cleared the table. If he did help, mom was always apologetic and grateful. I didn't see that I was duplicating my dad's expectations of what constituted a good marriage, into my own marriage. You know, it's like monkey see, monkey do. I guess I just emulated what I saw. When my wife explained her unhappiness to me, it didn't register. It didn't compute. I got angry and I got hurt. I became defensive and probably destroyed what might, now in retrospect, have been repaired. It's now only two years after our divorce was final that we've even been able to communicate at all. I finally understand what I did that contributed to her disappointment."

His ex-wife Sandy, a forty-one year old bank manager offered her version, "After all the hurt and resentment, I can finally see where I went wrong, too. I was so thrilled to be in the relationship with him, I wanted to please him so much and have him fall in love with me, that I did things and took on jobs that I really didn't want to do, at least not forever. I invited him over and would always insist on cooking. When we were finished and he started to help clean up, I'd push him away sending him to relax in the den while I cleaned up and fixed dessert. I really did those things *then* because I wanted to. Once we started living together, I did his laundry, folded his clothes and proved I was the perfect woman. He praised me and lavished me with genuine appreciation and affection. The more I did, the more I got. I sort of became addicted to it. I was in love and this was the way love was supposed to be. After nine years of it, and the kids as an added responsibility, I started resenting him for letting me become so overloaded. I just withdrew my affection, one tiny piece at a time. Before I knew it, he returned the resentment I showed him, and it just grew and grew and grew. I knew where it was headed but I felt powerless to stop it."

"Since we've been divorced," Steve added, "I cook for myself and the kids when I have them. I clean up, vacuum, do my own laundry, it's no big deal. I think I've grown a lot since the divorce. I wasn't as considerate in my marriage as I am now, but it never was that I didn't want to be, I honestly don't think I knew any better."

MISCONCEPTION #2: THINKING THAT OUR PARENTS' RELATIONSHIP WITH US OR EACH OTHER DOES NOT AFFECT OUR OWN ADULT RELATIONSHIPS

Many of us struggle to emulate what we saw and experienced while living with our parents, and many disavow it completely. Either way, our parents' relationship left an indelible mark on each of us. Whether or not we fully understand how and why, our own relationships as adults are indeed impacted by the relationships of our parents. Unbeknownst to our conscious being, we carry many preconceived ideas and expectations right into the new relationships we have so much hope for. When we fall in love we're essentially attempting to recapture the memories of the idyllic state of connection between mother and child. We assign that sense of peace, trust and belonging to our new partner. That's why we often attribute that sense of well being that overtakes us at the beginning of a love relationship, to our partner. "He makes me feel so loved, so wanted." "He makes me feel so safe, I don't think I could ever be happier." "He makes me so secure, I'm in a good mood all the time."

This is the wonderful part of love, but it's also unwittingly setting us up for disappointment. Whether our parents were wonderfully nurturing or severely neglectful or anything in between, we *associate* the way we felt back then and equate (actually, *confuse*) it with now. Of course this is never done consciously, it happens somewhere down deep in the recesses of our brain. For example, if we have been wounded as a child, we possibly have become overly wary. If we felt ignored or unloved, we may be overly clingy and look for too much reassurance from our mates. If we were smothered and fretted over, we may unconsciously be pushing our partners away or *we may be victim of our partner transferring those feelings onto us.*

"We all have the Great One Who Got Away," said Ralph, a thirty-one year old grocery store manager. "I really didn't mean to push Gail away. I never realized how much I withdrew once we were living together. She tried to get close, and the closer she came the further back I went. It wasn't like that in the beginning, but once we were living together and thinking of marriage I just didn't seem to be able to help myself. She stayed four years and before she left, in a confrontational scene I never want to repeat again, we were screaming horrible things at each other. But one of the last things she said was that I needed professional help. She said my mother was a control freak and that I was getting back at my mother through her. She hated my mom during the relationship, so I just discounted what she said while screaming, and I guess I discounted it all through the relationship. When my last girlfriend left after almost two years, saying the exact same thing, I realized I had better think seriously about this.

"The hardest thing I've ever done in my life was making that first appointment to see a therapist, but it was one of the best things I've ever done. I've learned to see that the women I cared for the most, I really was pushing away. I never brought to the surface how much I hated the way my mother always had to know everything and be included in every part of my life. She never gave me privacy, and all during those wasted years, I was getting back at her by making the women in my life feel isolated and uninvolved."

A toast to Ralph. He's actually one of those evolved people who had the courage to recognize a problem and, rather than sweeping it under the rug, sought answers. He can't change what happened to him, he can't change how it made him feel, but he can and *did* change how he is allowing it to affect his life today.

Chapter 15

Expectations- Identifying Yours And Sorting Reality From Fantasy

The real-life stories presented in the previous chapters, and hundreds more just like them, illustrate that unconscious expectations run amok on both sides. The insecurities, dysfunction and vulnerabilities created by our past can be avoided *prior to a relationship*, if both parties simply take the time and effort necessary to learn how to identify their own expectations and behavior patterns... and those of a potential partner. Most of us have never known that this was necessary, believing if we love someone enough, or that once a relationship was settled, everything would fall into place.

In our lifetime, divorce, or simply picking up our marbles and leaving a relationship, has been made easy, but it is not the answer to an unhappy union. People have come to think that when things get tough, the tough just get going—merely change partners and wash all your blues away. Somehow we have been given a misguided message: if you want to grow and change, simply exit your relationship.

Well, guess what? Singledom is filled with people who have been married three, four and even five times and/or had as many relationships. We're all gifted when it comes to giving our friends advice, but how many of us are lucky enough to see our own situations with the same clarity? If you don't figure out what your expectations are, and then examine those of a potential mate, you could marry as many times as Zsa Zsa Gabor and still never have even one relationship flourish. Marrying so many times and never enjoying sustained happiness is, for me, a horribly scary proposition.

We enter into relationships with monetary expectations, with achievement expectations, social and family expectations and a steam trunk worth of baggage from the past. Establishing sustained happiness has nothing to do with money, the color of your eyes or your dress size. It's the way you learn to live your life. Understanding how to correctly communicate and coexist with the important people in your life is what will bring you protracted joy, not just intermediate satisfaction.

There is an exercise you can do to determine recurring relationship problems that will give you hindsight that is almost 20/20. First, on a sheet of paper list each and every love relationship that you had high hopes for, but that ultimately disintegrated. (It is not necessary to list the short term dating relationships unless they were significant.) I know it sounds like another seemingly silly exercise (like beating up a chair with a pillow to tell your father you're angry at him because he didn't take you to the father-daughter ping-pong match when you were seven,) but it works.

Then, on a separate sheet of paper, or several, write the following twelve questions, leaving ample space between each to write your answers:
- How did I feel at the beginning of this relationship?
- What attracted me to this person?
- What made me fall in love with him?
- What needs of mine did he fill?
- What needs of his did I fill?
- I remember really being happy in the relationship until?
- What is the first thing I remember going wrong?
- What were the things we were constantly arguing or disagreeing about?
- What were the things he was constantly criticizing me about?
- What things did I constantly criticize him about?

✍ *How did it end?*
✍ *Was there anything that I thought could have saved the relationship?*

Now make as many copies of this master as you have listed relationships. At the top of each page list one name and the time you were involved together: Albert Smith, college, junior year 1981 - 1982. Do this for each of those relationships. Now go back and put them in chronological order. Of course, traveling down memory lane will take some time, but the trip will provide eye-popping perspective on your past.

What did you discover? Are you constantly falling in love with someone's potential only to discover they never live up to it. Are the men you are involved with controlling and do problems arise whenever you assert yourself? Are you overly nurturing and do you end up mothering the men in your life and running yourself ragged in the process? Are you trying to recreate your father or are you running from him right into the arms of the exact opposite? Ask yourself questions until you can see if you have developed any patterns.

If every time you eat an apple it gives you indigestion, isn't it safe to assume apples may not be good for you? You didn't die, but you certainly don't feel good either. If you're not having success establishing relationships at all, or if every relationship you have brings you some kind of misery, isn't it safe to assume that the course you are following, hoping to get to the promised land, is off-kilter somewhere?

It is only when we desire to change and break free from ingrained patterns that we can begin to understand how to make the right choices for ourselves and keep from making the same mistakes over and over again. Just as Ralph finally decided to discover how his past infringed on his potential for happiness in the present, all you need to do this successfully is the willingness to learn, the determination to understand what you uncover, and minimally, to entertain the idea that there just might be a better way.

Chapter 16

Expectations Are Like Lips:
Everyone Has Them. It's What You Do With Them That Counts!

The previous chapter offered a glimpse of expectation gone awry undermining relationships; this chapter puts expectation in perspective. Women are always being accused of trying to change and mold men, of falling in love with their potential. But when expectation is utilized correctly, the outcome can be surprisingly positive.

My friend Elaine is continuously getting herself involved in relationships that most of her friends clearly see as impossible. She always picks out a good man, but then starts to mold him right away. In the beginning they're fascinated by her. High power job, articulate, bright, funny. She's wonderful to be around. Then she knows someone who can get the guy a better job or classier suits at discount. She starts insisting they work out together. "Eat bran flakes," she told her last boyfriend, a forty year old airline pilot; "Frosted Flakes are so-o childish, and besides," she added for good measure, "too much sugar; you'll be sleepy in an hour and you'll crave sweets all day."

"Not too swift telling this to a guy first thing in the morning," say the people who love her. The boyfriend moved out two weeks later. Not that it matters, but he took his Frosted Flakes with him and left her his jogging suit.

The boyfriend before the pilot was an auto mechanic. This time she had the key to happiness. Why was she "wasting so much time on these self-centered professional types?" she asked everyone who'd listen. "A man doesn't have to have a Ph.D. to make me happy," she proclaimed. "Jeff really knows how to pay attention to me. He takes the time to do the little things." Yeah. That was before she lined up every car in the neighborhood in need of a piston, tune-up or spark plug for him to fix. Nights and weekends, there were so many cars parked in front of her house it looked like the parking lot at Woodstock.

"I'm just helping him get ahead," she said. "You know, make some real extra money." We swear Jeff went under a car one day and just never came out. He was never heard from again. Try as you might to help, some people just won't want to see the forest for the trees.

"Mindi," she called me bright and early one Saturday morning. "You'll never guess what."

"Grrr-ugh," I replied still essentially asleep . "I know what's been wrong all along. I've been afraid to admit it to myself, but not anymore," gushed Elaine.

For this I perked up. "That's great, Ela–yre–n," I said yawning. "Did some soul searching, huh?," I asked.

"Yes," she admitted, "and it was so obvious. I don't know why I didn't see it before."

It was like waiting for the other shoe to drop. "What?" I wanted to scream, but didn't. I could feel her leading up to something big, something profound and I didn't want to spoil it for her.

"I'm going to go blonde," she announced like she was stating the discovery of the cure for cancer. "I don't know why I haven't done it before now. All those blondes on the Ultress boxes look so happy, so content."

"So do the brunettes," I said with what I hoped sounded more like conviction instead of shock.

"The blondes are smiling more," she insisted. "Look at Meryl Streep, Michelle Pfeiffer, even Madonna for crying out loud, they always look so happy," she was almost yelling.

"You'd look that way too if you got two million dollars a film," I rebutted. I was obviously not reacting as she had hoped.

"People have said it for years," she proclaimed, mustering her final closing argument. "Blondes simply have more fun. Go back to sleep," she added. "You're grumpy this morning."

"I could also be Sleepy, Dopey and Doc. Being blonde isn't going to make you more content," I pleaded. With that she hung up. I saw her four days later as she was chasing me down the aisle of a mall and I was running away as fast as I could. I didn't recognize this nut who was flailing her arms and chasing me. She caught me easily, all those workouts and bran flakes, I suppose.

"It's me-e," she shrieked as she took off her sunglasses. I knew the voice but not the Loni Anderson "do". "It's me, Elaine, silly."

"Huff, puff, huff, puff, Oh God," I whimpered, still obviously out of breath and out of my mind trying to think of what in the hell to say to her next obvious question, which came like a bullet right on cue. "Don't ya just love it?" Thank goodness she didn't give me time to answer as usual. Instead, she started telling me about all the men who were flocking to her. "It's incredible. Men I've worked with for years, men on the street, even the toll takers. It seems like everyone. Actually women, too," she said, now sounding a wee bit puzzled. "I'm happier than I've ever been."

At this point I started to notice her making eye contact with perfect strangers walking in the other direction. She even said "Hello," once or twice. SHE WAS SMILING AT ALMOST EVERYONE. We stopped for lunch and she made idle chatter with the waitress. On her way to the ladies' room she stopped to tell the manager how nice the meal was. We went to my favorite book store and she was even nice to the sales clerk.

After the mall, I got busy with a deadline and we didn't see each other for a month or so. She called and we made plans to go to dinner the following week so I could meet the boyfriend du jour. "This is Robert," she said glowing from head to toe. From the very beginning I knew something was different, but I couldn't quite put my finger on it. After making small talk at the bar for a few minutes, he said he was going to ask the maitre d' how much longer until our table was ready.

She said, "Fine." Just *FINE*, I said to myself? No instructions, no discussions. Just FINE?

When we were finally seated and deciding what to order, she asked, "What's everyone eating?" Okay, here it comes, I thought. She's going to shoot him out of the air like the Red Baron. Then he said, "I think I'm going to have...," dead silence that seemed an eternity filled the air, as I squinted for impending doom, "...the quiche and a Caesar salad," he said. Oh no, I thought. Bad dog. Bad dog. Real men don't eat quiche, don't you know that?? I braced for the worst and accidentally kicked him under the table at the same time. "Oops, sorry," I muttered.

"Hmmm, quiche" she said. "Sounds good, I think I'll have that too."

I THINK I'LL HAVE THAT TOO?

She never had anything, TOO! What about the eggs, the fat, the cholesterol... and the little baby chickees who sacrificed their lives for that frivolous quiche?!", I screamed internally. When they made her blonde they must have sucked out the old Elaine and inserted a Stepford wife. Maybe they have her real personality in some incubator like the hearts they wait to transplant.

About then it dawned on me, (my "Why Factor" theory confirmed once again). She thought that the blonde hair was attracting people to her when in fact, *she* was being more outgoing and more friendly. She was less judgmental and more loving than I'd ever seen her. She had an expectation of what being blonde was going to do for her, when in fact, she unwittingly was projecting the image she believed the hair projected. Psychobabble aside, Sigmund would be proud of me, but she didn't have a clue. It had nothing to do with the color of her hair. It could have been punk-rock purple, it was her *self confidence*, and her *attitude* that had undergone the change.

As she leaned over and kissed Robert on the cheek for saying yet something else brilliant, it occurred to me that expectations are indeed like lips—it's just knowing what to do with them that counts.

Chapter 17 | How To Choose Who's Right and Avoid Who's Wrong

In this chapter, my grandmother's "There's a cover for every pot" theory is strengthened. Sure you can put a cover on a pot that doesn't fit, but it either falls in and you waste time plucking it out and washing it clean, or it's too big and the steam escapes.

By and large, women spend too much precious time trying to make Mr. Somewhat Okay *into* Prince Charming. Wouldn't it be less traumatic to pick out the right guy first? It would if you knew what to look for and what things to steer clear of. But make no mistake, if you are on the hunt for Mr. Perfect, he does not exist. Just as you have faults, and what my grandmother called *schtick*, so do men.

I'm always amazed at the answers that singles, who are recently divorced or who have just left relationships, give when I ask what attracted them to their last partner.

"I met Jane on the ski slopes and she just looked so sexy in that purple ski outfit, she turned everyone's head. I knew at that moment that I was going to fall in love."

"When I met Jeff, he was the first guy who would spend hours talking about books with me. He knew the authors that I knew. He'd read the poems that I loved. I fell head over heels after our first afternoon together."

Excuse me, hello. Earth to daydreamers. What about the way he views religion, will treat your pet Akita, and feels about you meeting the girls for a drink once a week? Many times we fall in love with the fantasy of who we believe someone is or worse, who we want them to be. The horrifying reality is that people who enter into relationships because they fall in love with someone's spirit, physical package or essence, only know one small part of who that person really is. Unfortunately, six months, a year or five years down the road, they're starting this whole process all over again, hardly more informed than the first time.

Most people put care and thought into developing their resumes, yet they base with whom to have a relationship with on the fact that he has nice eyes, a great butt or that he's a "good catch." Money does not insulate you from heartache and incompatibility. Neither will a great set of baby-blues.

When we lose or leave a job, countless hours are spent reading the want ads, interviewing with employment agencies and networking with almost anyone who might put us in touch with the right job. And since we spend at least one quarter of our lives working, that's one of the smartest things we can do. Having the right job is an essential element adding to the quality of our lives and ultimate happiness. Isn't it worth dedicating at least as much time and effort into determining if a potential spouse is right for you, BEFORE THE RELATIONSHIP GOES TOO FAR? Precious few of us do that, but it's no wonder—*how can we be expected to do it if no one ever taught us how?*

Yes, yes, yes, you must have chemistry and a level of physical attraction. I would never profess to convince you otherwise. Wanting to tear someone's clothes off with your teeth is a powerful aphrodisiac and a great start on what could turn out to be the love of your life, BUT IT IS NOT ENOUGH, AND IF YOU THINK IT IS, YOU'RE BUILDING THE FOUNDATION OF YOUR DREAM HOUSE ON POPSICLE STICKS. It eventually will come tumbling down around you.

In order to create a lasting love, not just a lustful love, you must get to know your partner *intimately*, and I'm not talking in the Biblical sense here. I'm speaking *fundamentally*, otherwise your ego (and theirs) creates the illusion of love. And while you both may be enjoying this immensely addictive "honeymoon period," if you don't make a conscious effort to explore just who this person is, how they think, feel, eat, dress and squeeze the toothpaste, etc., etc., etc., determining *objectively* how this fits into *your* lifestyle plan, you're creating something called *conditional love*. A relationship conceived on conditional love disintegrates by teeny, tiny pieces each and every time you disappoint each other.

But how can you develop *unconditional* love?

First, by learning as much about *your own* wants, needs, goals, *realistic* hopes, dreams and desires as possible, and second, by discerning as much of the same information as you can about any potential Mr. Right and third, by understanding how to compare the two.

To begin, you need to do some self-discovery. "Ugh, yikes, yuck" I hear the internal screams coming from deep within you. "Didn't I already do enough painful self-discovery just rehashing and remembering all my unsuccessful relationships," you groan?

Yes, but you're only half-way there. That exercise was done to show you any patterns you may be recreating that doom your relationships; this exercise will be your first step towards insulating your future ones. Like the sneaker commercial says, Just Do It!

"I can't believe you're asking me these questions," said Bill a thirty-four year old attorney from Chicago. "I think getting in the army was easier than getting into *the Bachelor Book*. I don't remember ever taking the time to think about these things. They're great questions and I can see how they're vital to having a successful relationship but I'm just shocked that at almost thirty-five, I hadn't really given these kinds of questions much thought before."

Over the years at *the Bachelor Book* and *the Bachelorette Book* magazines, we devised an in depth formula for determining if an applicant would be a successful candidate for inclusion into one of the magazines. First, we developed a lengthy questionnaire and then, an accompanying set of questions utilized during our interview process that compel our bachelors and bachelorettes to better understand just who they are, where they're headed and what they really want from life, from a partner and from a relationship. It covers myriad fundamental issues as well as hopes, fears and temperament. We do this not to pass judgment on anyone, but to unearth important information that must be carefully thought through before determining a truly relationship-ready individual. And there are no right or wrong or politically correct answers. On the following pages is an excerpted version of the questionnaire we use to select candidates for our magazine. Photocopy them and put them away until you have an uninterrupted hour or so to concentrate. Don't try to read and mentally answer each one, you'll miss the whole point. Take your time, perhaps pour a glass of juice or wine and sit down with the papers, a sharp pencil and a clear head. **Be completely honest**, you're the only one who will ever see it, so your sole criteria is simply to execute the exercise truthfully. After you complete it, just hang on to it. Reading it over and thinking about it a couple of times would also be a plus and immeasurably helpful for your future. If you don't have the time to do it now, my suggestion is to stop reading the book until you do.

SELF DISCOVERY TEST:

What do you like to do for fun?
What's a great evening to you?
A dream vacation to me would be...
Doing what, makes you the happiest?
Describe yourself to someone who doesn't know you...
What do you consider to be your biggest asset?
What other five assets come in next?
How do you think others see you?
Do you think they see the qualities (assets) in you that you described?
If not, why do you think that's so?.

What are your goals?
What are your dreams, (fantasies)?
What are the three things you'd like to change about yourself.
Are you easy-going, hot-tempered or somewhere in between?
What sort of things get on your nerves?
What makes you the angriest?
What three things come next?
How do you handle your anger?
What's the easiest way for someone to reach and reassure you
    when you're hurt and angry?
The person I admire most is? Why?
The things I envy most are?
I'm most insecure when I'm?
I feel loneliest when I'm?
The one fear I try to hide most is?
The best thing about men is?
I view dating as...
What do you notice first about a man?
What do you look for in a man?
Make a list of all the separate qualities and why they are
    important to you.
What habits turn you off in a man?
What are the things you could not tolerate in a man?
What do you look for in a relationship?
What do you think you bring to a relationship?
What are the top five ingredients you think will make a
    relationship successful?
Are you able to successfully communicate your needs to a partner?
If yes, how do you do this?
If no, what do you think the reason is?
Are you open with your feelings or are you a hint dropper?
If there is something bothering you are you comfortable enough to
    just tell your partner or do you wait until he "discovers" it?
How would you like your partner to approach you if he thinks
    something is wrong?
Is there a part of your personality that people most frequently
    misunderstand?

Why do you think this happens?
Is there any alteration you could make to keep it from happening?
How do you handle criticism?
Would your past partners agree?
Would your friends and family agree?
What caused the demise of your last relationship?
How could it have been handled better?
What have you learned from your past relationships?
What things will you strive to do differently in a new relationship?
What's your biggest fear in a relationship?
Would you want a traditional relationship (woman works in home/man works outside it) or one where you worked outside the home too?
Do you expect a man to contribute to the household duties?
Are you neat or happily unorganized?
Do you become uncomfortable in a relationship?
When and why do you think that happens?
Have you ever felt "let down" in a relationship?
If yes, what do you think happened and why?
What does the concept of mutual respect mean to you?
Do you think there is any pattern to the partners you choose?
To me, love means...
The best thing about being in love is?
The worst thing about being in love is?
Are you close with your family?
Are you open and loving with your family?
Do you enjoy spending time with them?
Would it bother you if a man is close to his family?
What if he weren't?
Would it make you jealous if a man wanted to spend time with his family?
How much time would be adequate?
How much would be too much?
How do you expect a man to show he appreciates you?
Is religion important to you?
If your partner's beliefs were different, is that a problem?
Would it be a problem in the future?

What steps could you take to prevent it from becoming a problem?
Do you want children of your own?
If your partner already has kids, is this a deterrent to you?
Can you love a partner's children?
Do you think you might resent them over time?
What reasons would make you resent them?
What steps could you and your partner take to avoid this becoming a problem?
If you already have children, what expectations do you have of a partner with respect to how he treats your children?
To me, having money means?
Do you believe your partner has the potential to earn more than he's making now?
If he never did, would this bother you in the long run?
What do you think is the proper way to handle money in a relationship?
Do you consider yourself a spender or a saver?
What if a partner did not feel the same?
Are you a person who lives for the here and now, spending money freely, or can you only be secure when there is a cushion? How much of a cushion is necessary?
Are you looking forward to having in-laws or do you view it as problematic?
Are you a pragmatic person or are you emotionally driven?
Do you get angry if things don't go your way or can you be content to compromise?
How do you handle disagreements?

The questionnaire you just completed is a hybrid, yet very similar to those we use at the magazines to gauge whether or not an applicant is right for us and vice versa. By examining the answers, we became very adept at determining some very specific information about each candidate. For example, we look for men who are family-oriented and relationship minded, not simply out to fill a little black book. We seek women who want to love a man for who he is, not for what he can provide her with. We take the initial questionnaire answers and fuse them with the results of a rather lengthy telephone interview, thus bringing us closer to a fair and accurate assessment of the person we're interviewing.

Over the years we've received hundreds of letters from applicants saying they were amazed that we captured the very essence of who they are in their magazine profile to a much greater degree than they originally thought possible. We aren't only able to accurately offer insight into the applicant's heart and soul, but their fears, hurts, disappointments, desires, likes, dislikes, attitude, expectations and disposition. Discussing their fundamental feelings on children, (yours, mine and ours), family (are they close or distant), religion (spiritual or church-going and the degree of importance in their lives) and the type of relationship that would make them the happiest—traditional or shared responsibility, plus myriad other specifics essential to a relationship.

By doing our job well, we have initiated hundreds of weddings and long-term relationships by giving our magazines' readers a very precise, very specific glimpse of who the person they're reading about *really* is (picture included.) Doing so enables readers to find a solid match on many, many levels; a more solid foundation for a relationship than chemistry alone. In so doing, we inadvertently stumbled on a very workable formula enabling *anyone* to get to know another human being on those same all important fundamental levels: a boon to ferreting out hidden talents, kindness, integrity, care, concern and sensitivity. Our formula also signals areas to watch out for that could potentially be problematic if they weren't disclosed prior to a relationship.

By conducting our interviews in a non-judgemental, very caring way, even the so called "quiet ones" open up, paving the way for a remarkable depth in communication between people that ordinarily could take months or even years to explore. Many of our bachelors and bachelorettes have jokingly offered to *pay us*, commenting that the interview was like a cathartic therapy session, affording them a reason and the *time* to be genuinely reflective!

Now that you have spent some time writing out and considering your own answers to the questionnaire, I hope it gives you a clearer picture of your own fundamental issues. Isolate the ones you can live with, those you can't and those you might be willing to compromise on.

In ordinary life you can't sit down with a clipboard and pen and start firing the questions at each new man you meet, so how can you get the information you need? By developing a way to talk to them so they **want** to talk to you.

Saying things like "my friend Barbara and her husband Joe are always fighting about money. She wants to have a separate account, he thinks she's being selfish. How do you think a couple should handle money matters? Or "my cousin Myra and her husband are always arguing over his family. He wants to have dinner with his family every Sunday, she thinks that's overkill. What do you think is a workable solution to spending time at each other's parents' homes."

By talking about other people and using the situations that would be very important to you, you will gain valuable insight into how this man really thinks and feels. Without him feeling like he's being interrogated by the KGB. Doing this successfully and then learning how to examine the results to determine common interests, character, integrity and his potential to be Mr. Right is what will bring you that much closer to finding him instead of settling for Mr. He's-Gonna-Give-Me-Heartache.

Having taken the time to fill out the self-discovery questionnaire, you can see that it does indeed make you aware of many things that you haven't really spent too much time considering. Most of these things are not so important at the beginning of a relationship, but become paramount in the long haul. Little habits like being unorganized is cute and tolerable in the beginning, after a few years it can become the fuse that ignites the domestic atomic bomb. Working many of these topics into everyday conversation isn't that difficult. You can always use the questionnaire to assist you in remembering specific topics. You can bring different subjects up at random. Some men, many men in fact, are interested in self-discovery and would welcome an opportunity to bring fundamental issues out into the open, up front. People who really want to get into a healthy, fulfilling relationship know that discovering how a potential life-mate really feels could save years of heartache and misery.

While conducting these interviews for our magazines, we always find it interesting how adamant some applicants are about a lot of issues they deem fundamental, but really aren't. On the surface, having a good understanding of what issues bother you is excellent. However, on some issues, compromise might be the wiser option.

Amy is a twenty-six year old non-smoker from San Diego. "I really value health and taking care of myself. I'm a graphic artist and I work for a company that has a `no smoking in the building' policy, which is fine with me. I met Alan when he moved into my apartment building and we became instant friends. I never considered getting into a relationship with him because I met him with a cigarette in his hand, and I made that clear to him. As I got to know him without the pressure of a possible relationship, I started falling in love with him. Our families were similar, he was a great cook, we both love animals, I could go on and on. We had so many similar interests, and around me he was what I call a considerate smoker, going outside my apartment if he felt like a cigarette, never smoking in the car or during dinner in a restaurant. It took six months and I was head over heels. The first time he kissed me he had been gone about two minutes. He knew he was going to kiss me and he went and brushed his teeth! Suddenly, it's not such a big deal, he's so wonderful in so many other ways."

HOW TO AVOID WHO'S WRONG
FUNDAMENTAL ISSUES:
1/ Family

Is he on a par with you in terms of how you each relate to your families? For example, if a person rarely sees or speaks to his family, it sends up at least a pink flag to us at the magazine. We wouldn't necessarily eliminate him, simply probing further to determine if his parents were abusive, if he had a bad childhood and the toll the effects took on him. On a personal level, if you're very tight with your family and you become interested in establishing a relationship with someone who doesn't or can't relate to that, it can become the source of immeasurable friction or vice versa, unless a workable solution is discussed.

2/ Children

If you have kids, you need to determine how a potential partner really feels about them. Not just for a Sunday in the park but for at least eighteen years of Sundays in the park. Everything is always rosy in the beginning. You must be wise enough to realize he may be crazy about you but if he can't tolerate your children, you won't have a snowballs chance in hell of making the relationship last. The same is true in reverse. If the child support he pays, the time he spends with his kids, or the patience he shows them in person or on the phone makes you angry or jealous in any way, it's time to reconsider the long range ramifications. Also, if you or he desperately want your own children, it better be addressed up front when it feels like the relationship may be deepening. If one does and the other can't or won't and the choices are not clearly discussed and understood, one or both parties will end up feeling, hurt, angry and cheated. People's feelings are not often swayed in this department. What's the sense of becoming involved with someone only to run into this stumbling block down the road? Sweeping subjects like this under a rug, hoping that once a relationship is in progress, the bond will become so tight your partner will change his mind, is foolish. That's the ostrich syndrome. Not dealing with the situation doesn't mean it will disappear.

3/ Money

How couples handle and manage finances is one of the most frequent, recurring problems in relationships. Some couples view money as the scepter of power in a relationship, always trying to wrestle control from the other. Some just view it on different fundamental levels, one seeing it as a source of pleasure, deserved rewards for hard work, having an I-can't-take-it-with-me attitude, while the other may view it on the same level with having locks on their doors—the very essence of safety and security. Instead of spending on a nicer car, a swimming pool, a great vacation or a gold bracelet, they stockpile it like a squirrel storing nuts before winter. One may be a whiz at managing, organizing and planning, the other only remembering to pay a bill when a guy in a trench coat shows up at the door with another guy named Guido. Having separate accounts may give one partner a sense of independence and emotional security and the other may view it as a wedge driving them apart. It's especially cumbersome when one partner has so much more than the other going into a relationship. Or when you're older and have separate grown families who add to the pressure. As difficult as it may be initially, really sitting down and talking turkey is the only way to insulate your relationship from the avalanche of problems money (or the lack of it) can create.

4/ Religion

For most of us, religion is either an issue or it isn't. I'm Jewish; my husband is Catholic. We have a real nine-foot Christmas tree every year with a Menorah on top. To us, that was as deep as the conflict over differences went. Religion is a very integral part of many people's lives, and when it is, they rightfully want to share it with a mate, and if they have children, they want to pass their religious beliefs on to them. To others who don't practice, it may not be as big an issue... until they have kids, or their parents exert pressure. Whatever category you fall into, it is of monumental importance to discuss this with someone. It may not bother you in the beginning if someone does not share your enjoyment of Sunday service, but five years from now it might, and then it's too late.

5/ Home and Hearth or Social Butterfly?

"I had to make an appointment with my ex-wife's secretary just to have dinner with her," joked Dan, a forty-seven year old high school textbook writer. "But under the surface I was fuming. She was the co-chair of this luncheon or that dinner, she was buried in meetings, seminars and dining with clients. Almost every night of the week she has a club or function to attend. I loved that she had her own interests when we met, but in the five years we were married, I think she took it to extreme. On Saturdays, she runs all the errands she didn't have time for during the week. Then for dinner, she always had us going out with the new neighbors, people from work or people she met somewhere. On Sundays, she was paralyzed—so tired she slept most of the day. I knew she loved people and being in the limelight. In the beginning, I thought it was exciting to be with someone who was always so much in demand. Now I realized what a mistake I made thinking that. I'm more reserved, I like being home watching a movie, snuggling on the couch, making dinner for just the two of us. I like talking by the fire, but just her and me, not with twenty-six of our closest friends. It just wasn't her thing. We're still friends, but it just didn't work. I understand just how important lifestyle compatibility is now. I just wish I would have understood it better six years ago when we first met. We both would have been saved a lot of hurt and pain."

This is an area we are just starting to take into consideration. Years ago, it was a *given* that men's lives were always the full ones, they were the ones finding time to squeeze *us* in. Now, as women's lives fill to the rim, how we spend our non-working hours has become a real concern. Some people like to celebrate TGIF by getting all gussied up and hitting the town, sleeping late Saturday, then doing it all over again. Others can't wait to exchange their briefcases and heels for fluffy slippers and a book and head straight for the sofa. If you can each make a concession to the other, you have the best of both worlds. If you can't, the friction will make your living room light up like the Fourth of July. If you choose the concession route, it's helpful to verbalize just how much of a concession each is willing to make. Don't just rely on "Sure I'll take you out." Is that once a week, once a month or once a millennium?

6/ Household Responsibilities

At the outset, this may not seem like a problem. The key to knowing if someone is right or wrong for you is ascertaining how your potential partner really views the prospect, independent of you doing all the cooking and cleaning in the beginning to prove your wonder woman. Do you prefer a traditional relationship where the man works outside the home and the woman within it? Or would you function better (or would finances dictate) where you each work outside the home and share the household responsibilities equally? First, you have to determine how you feel about this part of your relationship and what contribution each of you should make. What things can you tolerate, what things won't you? People often break this into "your job or mine," if that works, great. If you can't fathom putting a garbage pail out, make that understood, don't assume he'll just know and consider it his job. Just the same, if you can't stand that he throws your "good" leggings, spandex cat suit and thirty-two dollar bra in with the rest of the laundry instead of hand-washing them, tell him that laundry is a job you'd *prefer* to do and explain why.

Problems arise when we choose a partner whose feelings are fundamentally different from ours. Some men feel it only fair to share the work load if a woman works outside the home as he does. Others want a woman who will take full responsibility for the home and the children. Others, archaic as they may still and probably always will be, expect a woman who works outside the home to also take full responsibility for it. You have to figure out what role you want to play, making sure your partner's feelings don't conflict or infringe on your choice and vice versa. Opening up the avenues of communication, even on the most rudimentary levels at the onset of a relationship, will improve your chances of jumping any hurdles that may lie in your path.

LEARNING TO EVALUATE MEN

After dating even a short period of time, we begin to see

things in a person that we absolutely adore and other things that start to drive us up and over a wall. The problems start when we see blatant signs of characterisitics we don't like, things we disapprove of, or things that make us feel downright uncomfortable. Worst of all is when we ignore our little voice. When our intuition tells us to turn left not right, we're so grateful because turning right would have made us ten minutes late for the meeting. Yet, when the man we're dating yells at us for forgetting to buy sugar, we ignore the very same voice that's yelling *"danger! danger!"* Instead, we decide he's just tired and under stress. But, our intuition isn't selective. Sure our intuition sometimes goes into overdrive, sometimes making us jump to conclusions, but if we temper that intuition with the ability to examine other evidence before making a judgment, we can acquire some very accurate information on which to base an educated decision. Never is learning to do this more important than when you are thinking about whether or not the man you're involved with would be a good husband.

As women, we tend to nurture, therefore thinking we can fix anything. You can wipe up spilled milk, you can put a band-aid on a booboo, you can make the impossible deadline for presentation. What you can't do is fix every man you meet and you can't ignore the signs that tell you he's in need of repair. Of course, nothing is absolute. Yes, there is the lonely, sullen man that blossoms when he has the love and reassurance of a good woman, but no amount of love and assurance you give to a man who punches you or assaults you verbally when he's angry, will make it go away. That's a job only for a professional. The alcoholic will not throw the bottle away when you shower him with love and affection. The cheat will not be faithful once he finds a caring, deserving woman. The leopard that gets dirty when he plays in mud will be able to wash the mud off, but the spots underneath remain.

As a way of evaluating a man's potential to be a good, loving, long-term partner, ask yourself the questions listed below. If there are things you see emerge that you're little voice has been screaming to you for months, think long and seriously about what continuing to ignore the signs could mean to the rest of your life.

- How do you feel when you are with him?
- Does he make you doubt yourself and abilities?
- Does he constantly make "jokes" at your expense and then accuse you of being too sensitive?
- Does he make time for you or are you always having to ask him for attention?
- Does he make you feel guilty or needy ?
- Does he ever go out of his way to make you feel special?
- Does he speak to you with respect in public?
- Does he speak and treat you well in private?
- Do you feel like you're "walking-on-eggs" around him? What percentage of the time?
- Does he yell at you, even for minor infractions?
- Does he lose his temper at situations beyond his control?
- Is he always angry or ready to blow?
- Has he ever thrown or broken objects, hit walls or damaged possessions when angry?
- Afterwards, does he tell you *you've* overreacted to the situation and does he minimize his reaction while maximizing yours?
- Are you afraid that if you confront him he'll leave? Throw something? Hit the wall? *Or you?*
- Does he use even the most minor of incidents to get into a bad mood?
- Is he in a bad mood most of the time?
- Does he treat others well?
- Does he constantly criticize your friends or your family?
- Are you comfortable bringing him to family/social functions or are you always worried there'll be an incident or problem?
- Does he get along with his family?
- Does he treat his mother or sisters with respect?

- Does he love his family?
- Does his family love him or are they wary of him?
- Does he constantly criticize others, calling people stupid or inept?
- Does he get angry or testy with animals? or children?
- Does he abuse alcohol or drugs?
- Does he lie to his boss, co-workers, friends and family to get out of anything sticky?
- Does he shirk responsibility?
- Does he pay his bills?
- Has he borrowed money from you?
- Does he moan about money all the time?
- Does he ever buy you little gifts?
- Is he dependable, being where he says he is? Or do you always have a "sneaking suspicion?"
- Is his behavior consistent or erratic?
- Does he have close friends?
- Is he close to his kids?
- Is he a good, patient father?
- Does he say negative things about marriage?

IS THIS A MAN YOU COULD PICTURE YOURSELF SPENDING THE REST OF YOUR LIFE WITH?
How To Choose Who's Right

Feeling comfortable enough to talk about fundamental issues and discuss differences of opinion is a wonderful place to start. A man who cares for you won't begrudge some healthy conversation. When you read through the *How To Avoid Who's Wrong* list, you can see a great many of the areas that should serve as a giant red light. *A man who's right for you is a man who makes you feel accepted, respected, equal and whole.* Someone who supports you in your endeavors and doesn't have the need to belittle you in order to make himself feel better. A man who loves you is a man who isn't afraid to tell you when you're going off the deep end, and he's a man who'll be there to yank you back if you do. He's a man who protects you but doesn't smother or squelch you, and that's not to say he won't disappoint you, piss you off, get on your nerves and make you want to club him to death from time to time.

A man is not required to bring home little gifts to prove he cares, it's the gifts he gives you everyday: the encouragement, the added confidence, the benefit of what he knows and believes is best for you and the feeling that this man is adding a real dimension to your life.

But sometimes that guy is not Tom Cruises's clone. "Oh, God," remembered Marge. "The date was just dreadful. In the first six minutes he knocked over the drink of the man sitting next to him at the bar. The next calamity was spilling soup on his tie. It was obvious he was becoming more nervous and sweat started to bead on his top lip and obviously on his palms because he dropped the fork with a major clang. I was secretly vowing to put a contract out on my sister for arranging this date. Just as I was about to say, 'hey look, thanks, but no thanks,' his beeper went off. I was almost relieved until he told me it was his ex-wife and that his son was at the emergency room and since he didn't have time to take me all the way home, would I mind going along. I almost opted for a cab, but we were way out in the suburbs. At the hospital, he was incredible. The minute the little boy set eyes on him, he stopped crying and stopped being afraid. He had fallen and broken his arm and the doctor was about to set it. He seemed to put his son, his ex-wife, the doctor and me at ease. On the drive home he apologized, saying he knew the evening was a complete disaster. I invited him in for coffee and cake (since we hadn't had dessert) and we talked for hours about kids, life and how awful first dates can be. When I was able to see him in a different light it was apparent that this was a really wonderful man."

I have interviewed hundreds of men whom I call diamonds in the rough. Men, who only need to blow-dry their hair back instead of the way they wear it to the side. Men who wear black socks with sandals, or a polka dot shirt with a pair of old leisure suit pants. Men who are charmers once you get to know them, but couldn't come up with a line of clever repartee in a singles' bar if you held a gun to their head. Men who may have a ding or a dent but who also have the heart, sincerity and the inner character to make a woman feel loved, safe and happy. Men who don't set conditions for their love, but love unconditionally. Judging a book by its cover has become an Olympic event. In the kooky world we live in, we may be putting too much pressure on ourselves in the pursuit of perfection to the detriment of solace.

Sometimes a subscription to *Gentleman's Quarterly* is all it takes to equalize the two.

Chapter 18

Closeness and Commitment:
The Truth About How Men *Really* Feel

"Men really don't want to commit," says Colleen, a thirty-seven year old technical writer. "They say they do, but they really don't."

"Paul and I have been dating about six months and he is so wonderful 90% of the time. We have great fun together, we share so many of the same interests, we laugh a lot, but he freezes up and gets so distant when I want to talk about us and the future," said Rita, a twenty-nine year old flight attendant. "I just want to feel close, like we're headed in the same direction, but he gets so defensive."

"Can you tell me why, after over a year and a half in a relationship," said Lucianne, a beautiful thirty-five year old statistician, "did Roger become engaged to Traci (thirty-four) only nine months after he broke up with me? He's doing all the things he'd never do with me. I can't understand it. It wasn't like we didn't have a good sex life, or that we fought all the time. I just couldn't get him to *commit* to me. I seemed to have trained him for her."

"My last girlfriend accused me of not being sensitive to her, not showing how I felt about her and the relationship," said forty-one year old Brian, a commercial artist. "When I came home before her, I'd have dinner waiting. When she had a headache, I'd rub her neck until my hand fell off so she could fall asleep. When she was tired, I'd run a bubble bath or massage her feet. But none of that seemed to count. She wanted words. I guess I couldn't come up with the right words. She left me saying 'I want a commitment now. I need to know how you feel.' Aren't those things showing her how I feel?"

COMMITMENT - WHERE THE WIRES CROSS

There is no subject among singles as hotly debated as the topic of commitment. I have yet to speak to a group of singles where the topic hasn't come up, and when it does, everyone is fiercely passionate about their opinions. Just what is commitment and why does the mere mention of the word elicit such powerful emotions from both men and women? Emotions and ideas that appear to be diametrically opposed.

Webster, of dictionary fame, defines *commitment* as either "a pledge" or "a promise"; (ah, how sweet) or "the official consignment to a P-R-I-S-O-N or M-E-N-T-A-L H-O-S-P-I-T-A-L"!! (Good grief. It's a wonder any one gets married.)

Every single man and woman has a voice on the subject and a war story or two. "Men are commitment phobic," remarks one thirty-six year old woman who's been involved in four serious relationships, none of which has lead to marriage. I'm beginning to think the only way a man will get married is if you book the church, invite the guests, order the flowers and his tuxedo, and when he pulls up, just say, 'Here, put this on,' before leading him down the aisle."

"Men want their cake and to eat it too," offers another woman who said she feels used by men and then discarded, as they move on to the next.

"Women are so concerned with commitment down the road, they forget about enjoying the relationship in the present," says a forty-five year old tile company executive. "When I'm dating a woman only four or five months, how can I know what the future holds? I don't have a crystal ball."

The subject of a lasting commitment is a pivotal discussion

in most relationships. The outcome decides if the relationship will prosper and grow or wither and die.

Most women seem to feel that men shy away from commitment. Yet if that were true, why do hundreds upon hundreds of men come to *the Bachelor Book* each year looking to find someone to commit to? Most men feel that women are so preoccupied with commitment, that even the most secure woman becomes needy and commitment-hungry once she's in a relationship.

There is a cavernous disparity in the way women believe men think about commitment and the way men actually feel. The same holds true in reverse. So where did this inconsistency come from, and why do some people get just to the brink of commitment, yet never beyond it?

IMPACT OF HISTORY AND TRADITION ON MODERN PERCEPTIONS

One possible explanation for the perception of men as commitment shy lies in the history of our culture. Prior to the Women's Movement, a woman's worth was largely determined by the man she married. She had precious few other options, therefore women were indeed preoccupied with *snagging* a "good husband."

'Mrs. Shapiro's daughter married a doctor.'

'God bless her. Did you know that Mrs. Murphy's daughter Bridgett is engaged to the Butcher's son?'

In the movie *Fiddler on the Roof*, three young sisters sang, "matchmaker, matchmaker make me a match. Find me a find, catch me a catch. Night after night in the dark I'm alone, so find me a man all my own." Tzeitel, Hodel, and Chava were young women eager to start their lives, and to do so meant acquiring a husband.

Mothers passed esoteric advice to their daughters—marry well, and you'll have a good life. Words that have an indelible impact on the way we feel today, flowed from their lips, indoctrinating us all.

"He's a good *catch*."
"Your sister *landed* a good man."
"Even homely cousin Evelyn *hooked* one."
"Can you believe the divorcee down the block *corralled* another one?"

Men were talked about as if they were prey that women needed to set a trap for. We may joke about it, but that sentiment endures, and to some extent, has shaped our opinions, and to a lesser extent, our actions. In a sense, it's as if both sexes were brainwashed to varying degrees on parallel, yet vastly disparate, tracks. Men understood their role as provider and therefore as sought after husband material. Women understood—the better his income, the better *her* life.

Today, women need not marry to begin a life, to put a roof over their head or to even to start a family. In her book, *Single Mother's by Choice*, author Jane Mattes provides practical advice and support for women who decide that their biological clock can't wait for Prince Charming to arrive. Women who want a child *whether or not* they have a husband.

Was this even an option thirty years ago?

As significantly as we have progressed as independent women, and as many options as are now open to us, marriage still remains the last bastion of *making it* for the many women locked between the accomplishment oriented vitality of today and the traditional you-are-what-you-marry of yesterday. Many women still wear *marriage* as a badge that says, "Yes, world. Someone loves me. Someone *really* loves me." We grew up in a world that viewed men as the prize and marriage as the contest.

Is there any more truth to the *men-are-commitment-shy* theory generally held by women today, than there is in the perception men hold that *women are commitment-hungry?*

I think not. As has been pointed out many times throughout this book, the times indeed are changing, and so are the perceptions. The difficulty stems from living in the *midst* of these prodigious changes, meeting and falling in love with people that are in their own various stages of adjustment to those changes. If change were white, and tradition were red, it would be easy to identify who felt which way and then act accordingly. The problem remains that we now have thousands of shades of pink to contend with as well.

I have met and interviewed far too many men who relish making a commitment to accept the theory of them as commitment shy. In fact, according to a 1991 survey in the Los Angeles Times, Dr. Joyce Brothers reported that for the first time in 10,000 years, men regard having a wife and a family as more important than a career.

They simply won't make a commitment unless they feel *close*. Therein lies the second reason I believe the commitment disparity exists. The word *close* has a very different meaning to a man than it does to a woman.

CLOSENESS - IN THE EYE OF THE BEHOLDER

"It seems that once the dating relationship is moving towards something more serious, it starts to get complicated and out of sync. Everything is wonderful until the subject of commitment starts to creep into every conversation—either directly or with one lightly veiled hint after another. And it's happened with more than one girlfriend. Suddenly I feel like nothing I do is right. I'm always afraid of saying the wrong thing," said Jeff, a thirty-two year old computer programmer with the U. S. government. "When I'm quiet, I'm always accused of putting up a wall and not sharing my feelings. When I really make the effort to lighten up a situation with a joke or try to be playful, I'm told I'm sarcastic or deliberately trying to change the subject. I can't win. So I keep my distance, emotionally. I do want a committed relationship, but I don't want to get *close* to someone who's always telling me I'm doing something wrong. Don't women understand how this makes a man feel? They may constantly want to know where the relationship stands, I don't."

"Some women seem to constantly push men for a commitment," says Neil, a forty-nine year old stock analyst. "Or at least that's the kind of woman I seem to be meeting. I just broke up with a gal I had been seeing for about five months.

She was always saying 'Let's just sit and talk. I want to feel *close* to you.' Closeness is not something you invoke by talking. To me, it's something that *happens*. A feeling that develops by doing things and experiencing things together... over time. I feel closest to a woman who takes the time to allow me to bond with her. And for me that means doing things together, making memories or having adventures. Nothing has to be said or measured or decided. It's by becoming the absolute best of friends first. It's a natural progression, not a planned event. She pushed, and I tried my best to comply because I wanted that relationship to work. I took her to ball games with me, invited her to share the things I enjoy. I offered to do things she enjoyed, but she kept pushing for talk, talk, talk until I felt strangled. Nothing other than constant discussions about the direction of the relationship would suffice. I walked away and I miss her, but I was starting to feel like a masochist."

"It seems to me," suggested Tim, a thirty-nine year old college professor from Vermont, "that with all the independence women have achieved, they're still basically needy. The messages I get loud and clear are: *I don't need you to open my door. You don't have to pay my check – I make more money than you do anyway, or I'm perfectly capable of fixing my own garbage disposal, thank you*, but when all is said and done, they are still looking for constant verbal reassurance in a relationship. Isn't this a mixed message like they always accuse us of sending? They give the illusion of being independent and all it implies, but when women are in relationships, they can't go two days without discussing its status. To me, it's all very perplexing, and confirmation that a woman's self-esteem has nothing to do with achievement. You can't get close to women today. The minute you do, you become an emotional whipping boy."

"Maybe I am commitment-phobic like my last girlfriend said. I don't know," offered Peter, a forty-three year old registered nurse from Birmingham, Alabama. "If making a commitment means having to constantly reassure the woman in my life that I'm Okay and the relationship is Okay, *everyday*, then I guess I'm commitment-phobic. It's frustrating, exhausting, and I simply don't function on that kind of emotional level. If things seem Okay, if the relationship is deepening and we're getting closer, why do women have to constantly *check* in words? It is a turn-off and I do end up walking away. Because I can't seem to find a woman who is really self-assured, does that make *me* commitment-phobic?" "To me, it seems like a major sign of insecurity when a woman needs to constantly monitor the direction and speed of a relationship," said a forty-four year old landscaper. "Don't women believe men think about the outcome of a relationship, too? We just don't have the need to verbalize it all the time."

"It's a continuing source of frustration to me when I'm told I'm not being sensitive to a woman's needs," says Anthony, a twenty-seven year old assistant book editor. "But what about my needs? Ellen had to know how I was feeling or thinking *all the time*. Those were *her* needs. My needs were just living day to day, and seeing where the relationship was headed. I respected the fact she wanted a direction for her life, but I didn't have any better answers than she might have had. How can you predict if a relationship will lead to marriage in four months or eight months or even a year? It's too soon to tell if we'll mesh on critical issues. I think those things get worked out over time. I can't guarantee our longevity with *words*. Close is what I *feel*. Sometimes I felt closest to her when we're just cooking dinner together. I can't commit to someone if I constantly feel pressured by them."

"The last woman I dated, liked art galleries," offered Eric a fifty-six year old commodities trader from Chicago, "so we went to one on the last date we had before we split. We walked from picture to picture, the way I thought you're supposed to do in a gallery. The whole ride home she was weepy and accusatory because I didn't hold her hand or stop and discuss each piece with her. If I was done looking at one and moved to the next before she did, she saw that, as a deliberate attempt to ruin the *closeness* of the day! To me, just being there and sharing the day with each other was being close. How can you feel close to a woman when every move you make is being so closely examined? Closeness is a state of being. Words won't solidify it, holding hands won't—even marriage can't."

Bob, an attractive thirty-one year old accountant put it this way: "Women don't seem to understand that in order for a man to want to make a commitment, he has to feel close, and closeness is a state of mind; it doesn't have to continually be studied. I feel closest to my girlfriend when we're just sitting around reading the Sunday paper—*not saying a word*. But if she detects that my mood has shifted or that I get pissed at something, she starts hammering me. What's wrong? Is it something I did? She immediately wants to have a state-of-the-relationship-address. The greatest gift I could give women is to understand that you don't have to talk all the time to feel close."

Literally thousands of men have explained to me that in order for them to commit to a woman, they must first feel close to her. "I can have a great sexual attraction to a woman," offered Joshua, a thirty-nine year old infomercial producer, "but unless I feel close to her, *emotionally close* to her, I know it will *never* proceed beyond the initial lust."

If that be the case, then why does it appear to women that men bolt at the first discussion of closeness?

"I don't think it's a question of bolting at the first discussion of closeness," said Ryan a thirty-four year old school teacher. "It's that I don't think most women understand that a man's meaning of *close* is different from hers. There's a fine line between a closeness that is beautiful and able to endure and one that is *confining*. I think I'm a typical guy. Monogamous, loyal and pretty normal. To me, and I assume most men like me, closeness is something achieved through shared experiences, not discussion.

"But if I love, respect and care for someone, I'll try to put myself in her place. I'll try to *make* myself more verbal and address those needs. But the problem is that most women aren't satisfied with *one* frank discussion on the subject. In my experience, which is limited to about six of what I call serious relationships, each time I indicated that yes, I was interested in at least a foreseeable future, each one of the women wanted *specifics*. I can't give specifics about the future. All I know is *the now* and how the now feels. If we've been dating a few months and if it feels good, if our relationship is deepening on many levels, if we seem to be compatible, I assume it will keep growing and becoming more profound, eventually leading to marriage. Most women have a need to address the subject daily. That's the part that drives me up a wall. And if you don't, they start getting moody, or dropping hints or bringing up the issue in little dribs and drabs *constantly*. That's when I get turned off, when I get moody and distant and when I start losing interest. It's also the point at which I'm accused of being afraid to make an honest commitment, which I think is very unfair. It might be convenient for a woman to blame me. It might make her feel better or give her something to gripe about with the girls, but it's simply untrue. Most women never want to look in the mirror and see if their behavior could be adding to the demise of their relationships. It's easier for them to blame men."

"I'm not a frivolous guy; in all of my relationships, I don't think I would have lost interest if that constant probing wasn't an ongoing source of irritation between us."

When we arrive at the where-is-this-relationship-going-crossroad, many women want confirmation that the relationship is indeed headed somewhere—namely, to the altar. And that's a very valid concern. We have every right to determine if we're wasting our time. The problem seems to be that men and women get their wires crossed at this point. It's that one-step-forward-two-steps-back-polka again. She pushes forward, and he starts to retreat. If men want closeness, and women want closeness, how is it that we feel polarized by the subject? Is it that men really don't want to make a commitment when it gets down to the nitty gritty? Again, my research indicates that men do indeed want a commitment, but they need to feel close first, and close to a man is NOT TALK.

Men have confided over and over again that the first step is for women to understand that in order for a commitment to take place, closeness and trust must bind a man to you.

Men say that closeness is not just proximity. You can be in the same bed as a partner and feel as lonely as if you were on a deserted island. Men say that closeness is not just familiarity. You can know that he eats his broccoli, only with lemon, and drinks his coffee, black with two sugars, and still not know him. Men say closeness is not physical. You can make wild passionate love to someone and still not feel close. Men say that closeness is not just companionship. You can do everything together and never feel more apart.

Men say that in order to have closeness you must have emotional intimacy. And emotional intimacy is based on trust, and trust is based on deep friendship, and deep friendship is shaped by *acceptance, unconditional love,* and *compatibility*—which men say develops by being together, *not by talking.*

It's rather like getting a present in one big box only to find out that you have to open six progressively smaller boxes to get to the good stuff. Some women instinctively know how to start at the beginning, giving a man what he needs in order to build up to emotional intimacy one small step at a time, until he feels close, secure and that he cannot imagine his future without her. Some less secure women aren't sure if they're doing it right, so they *ask* for verbal reassurance, which is Okay. It's when the reassurance is sought too frequently that it begins to cancel out the friendship, the love and the trust, little by little.

So, how can you have your needs met and still meet his?

UNDERSTAND THE DIFFERENCES BETWEEN MEN AND WOMEN

Women are verbal, intuitive creatures; men are logical, and event oriented, and relationships are emotional seesaws with men on one side, women on the other. Both seek the same end but by sorely different means. Oftentimes, they alienate each other in the process, leaving two people who may indeed care deeply for each other, very hurt and very confused. The man, thinking she's needy and commitment hungry. The woman, feeling she had the misfortune of getting involved with yet another commitment-phobic man. This happens too often. Is there anything that can prevent it?

Yes, by understanding *why* it occurs.

When women feel thirsty for the same type of emotional support that we readily give to our men, we often find ourselves feeling abandoned or that our men don't care about us as deeply as we care about them. One explanation is that women are accustomed to and therefore put greater stock in *verbal reassurance*. Whereas men routinely *show feelings* through actions.

"When I make dinner, and then tell her to go rest, that I'll clean up; aren't I showing her how much I care?"

"But he doesn't *say* he loves me."

He's showing you. If relationships are to flourish with less hassle, women must learn to elevate the *demonstration* of his affection through his actions right up there with the power of hearing it in so many words. That's how he's made.

Another reason men appear less sensitive is that we are asking them to draw on a part of themselves that for years society dictated they stifle. What a paradox. Remember when "macho" separated the men from the boys? It wasn't that long ago when emotional men were branded wimps. Now we ask them to be sensitive, emotionally available and *verbal*, and many, many of them *are* or *are in the process* of getting there.

As women, feelings and emotions come easy to us. We have a hard time comprehending that the same is not true for men. "How is it possible he doesn't sense how I'm feeling?"

"If he really loved me, he'd try harder to figure out what I'm thinking." He might, if he were as biologically capable of it as we are. Scientific study after scientific study has proven beyond all reasonable doubt that men's and women's brains are constructed differently. Not that one is superior to the other, simply that they are different, therefore giving each sex their own explicit set of strengths and weaknesses. In their landmark book, *Brain Sex*, geneticist Anne Moir and journalist David Jessel literally explode the myth that men and women are created equally by documenting the differentiation in the brains of men and women. Distinctly different brain structure resulting in marked differences in the way men and women think and process information. "For years behavioral differences have been explained away by social conditioning or hormonal differences," they write. Even now, the findings are not popular or politically correct. But they *are* scientifically correct and in trying to sort relationships, the findings are vital. For example, Moir and Jessel point out that women possess a superior aptitude for speech. That's why women generally have an easier time learning foreign languages and *communicating feelings*. We are also more fluent. "Speech defects and stuttering occur almost exclusively among boys," they say, and "six times as many girls as boys can sing in tune." The female's superiority in sensory stimuli accounts for what we call our "intuition," which essentially is our ability to read faces, interpret gestures, and pick up more tones than can a man. In relationships, that's why it seems that women are using some high-tech emotional radar and why men seem to be groping around in the dark with a flashlight with faulty batteries.

Male brains are adapted to better deal with *things*. Man's spatial ability is superior to ours which accounts for their innate proficiency for figuring out puzzles and reading maps. *(Perhaps the reason they can program the VCR with greater ease.)* Men are better able to see patterns and abstract relationships. They can better picture, alter and rotate objects in their mind than can most women, perhaps an explanation of why men dominate the game of chess. They have better hand-to-eye coordination which is a necessary element for playing ball sports.

The differences extend to other areas as well. Women see better in the dark, men in bright light. Men have better depth perception, yet because "women have more receptor rods and cones in their retinas," writes Moir and Jessel, "women have a wider peripheral vision." To deny these differences is to go on running up against brick walls, especially in matters of the heart. *Men: The Handbook* was written to promote more understanding and compassion between men and women, and I believe that understanding starts with recognition that we are not interchangeable. It is our warranted right to be treated as equals, but expecting men and women to think, feel, react and verbalize identically is what I believe is causing much of the confusion and the rifts between us.

All through our lives, we have cemented friendships with other women by confiding our hopes, dreams, and secrets to each other. The deeper the secret, the closer the bond. The verbal nurturing and comfort we give each other is what allows us to connect so deeply and completely with other women. How many of us have ever said to a best female friend, "If only you were a man, you'd be my ideal mate?" We draw strength and support from our female friends and family members and we readily offer the same in return. It's something most of us don't have to work at, it comes naturally, because biologically that's how we were created.

Men aren't so lucky in this department. They are certainly physically stronger than we are and hormonally more aggressive, but they don't yet understand the strength and emotional security that women draw from being verbally close to each other. To many men, being *verbally* open means being vulnerable, and vulnerability affirms weakness in their eyes. In primitive times, weakness meant death. Growing up, weakness was marked by the *sissy*. These feelings are *ingrained*, and although men may walk upright and carry a briefcase rather than a spear, their apprehension about showing emotion hasn't changed all that much over the last couple thousand years.

Addressed by the recent "Men's Movement" which finally gives real men, whether they eat quiche or not, a license to feel, cry and to get in touch, some men now *want* the same wonderful gift we have and take for granted—our ability to show emotion, free from judgment. I remember a teacher in grammar school telling a crying boy who fell off his bicycle not to be such a baby. The kid was bleeding! Is it any wonder this boy and thousands upon thousands just like him grew up suppressing how they felt? As frustrating and unfulfilling as needing and not receiving verbal reassurance from a man can be, I feel more compassion for them, rather than anger, when they don't show it.

Men are just now realizing how liberating showing emotions can be. We just have to be patient with modern man. What they've spent millions of years suppressing, won't surface overnight. We are light-years ahead of them in this department and we need to understand them and gently coach them, not condemn them when our needs in this area are not met. "People are still reacting to propaganda left over from the 'me generation,'" says Susan Page, author of *If I'm So Wonderful, Why Am I Still Single?* "Their attitude is 'I need to get my needs met, and that's the most important thing.' We've forgotten how to take another person's well-being into account."

In order to get on the same emotional plane as a man, in order to allow a man to feel emotionally close to you, which he must feel in order for him to commit to you, it is imperative that as a woman you don't confuse the facts: Men may walk like us and may look like us, but that won't enable them to think, feel and express themselves the way we do. And expecting them to, will result in needless frustration.

As we're learning to be more decisive in the workplace, they're learning to be more in-touch. It's equivalent to learning to speak another language. Most of us, at least in the beginning, carry around a book and look up what we don't understand. But after studying it for some time we develop the confidence to speak without needing the book. The same holds true for men with respect to their emotions and the ability to adequately express them, only there is no book to look up what they don't understand or to show them how to express what they do. They're groping along the best they can for the short time society has given men the green light on emotion. We'll all be compost before the next round of evolutionary changes elevate men to the same level of sensory expression. Just when we have the need to feel close to a man, our very action sometimes trigger a response in him that causes him to act indifferently, and then, by misreading his reaction, women zig, when it would have been best to zag, which sets up a domino effect of hurt and confusion.

A case in point is our need for verbal reassurance. It's probably the number two destroyer of relationships, after anger. Men have told me, complained to me, and moaned to me about how the constant probing what I call *emotional-temperature-taking*, of the relationship is the reason many become turned off and frustrated, and is the reason they assume that the women who do the asking, are needy, clingy and commitment hungry.

It is our nature to work through what bothers us by discussing it... over and over and over again. We readily call our friends and analyze, bisect and dissect. It makes us feel better. If two heads are better than one, then four can be just dandy—offering us perspective and focus. Men don't understand it; they can't relate to it, and what's worse, our forcing them to endure it and/or participate in it is what causes the adverse reaction. We want them to comfort us; they certainly might try the first few times, but if the need is frequent, most men will invariably walk away from a woman they deem emotionally demanding. They are simply not able to cope. They don't mean to intentionally hurt their partner, they are just not equipped to do what our girlfriends can do with a simple phone call. If you want a man to commit to you, this is just one of those imbalances you must learn to live with if you want to happily coexist.

Another of those imbalances is timing, which is the third reason I believe men and women's views on commitment conflict.

TIMING - HOW TO GET IN SYNC

"I got blasted by this woman I had been seeing about two

months," said Morris, a sixty-three year old widower from Manhattan. "I was so shell-shocked I just walked around for hours, going over every little detail in my mind. What did I do wrong? She accused me of setting her up for a collapse. Of planning to make her fall head over heels with me and then dump her. She called me a *misogynist*. I didn't even know what the word meant. I had to look it up.

"When I did, I was even more baffled. It said *having or showing a hatred or distrust of women*. Me, a nice, Jewish man who was in love with his wife until the day she died. I adore women. And do you know what my crimes were?," he continued. "I gave her things. Walking to her apartment, I'd pass a flower stand; I'd walk in and pick up a few carnations or a lily. I'd go past a bakery; I'd buy a cake or a Babka I knew she'd enjoy with coffee. I took her out to nice dinners. I'd surprise her with a bottle of her favorite perfume or a frame to put the new picture of her grandchild in—she threw that frame at me during the argument. And the argument all started when I told her that my son was coming to New York on business and he and I were having dinner the night he landed. She wanted to know why she wasn't invited. I told her it wasn't a big deal dinner, just a quick bite to catch up because my son didn't have much time.

"A flood of emotion and anger came pouring out. 'I thought we were keeping company,' she said. 'I thought our relationship was important to you. I thought we were headed in the same direction.'

"I thought so too, until she accused me of being ashamed of her, of not thinking she was good enough to meet my son, of toying with her. He'd only have a few hours, I just didn't think that would be the right time. Who'd believe she could act this way?

"I wasn't toying with her. I bought her those things because I wanted to make her happy, not to set her up or imply anything. I was thinking of her, and thinking highly enough to want to do something nice for her. There was no hidden meaning one way or the other, just like meeting my son was not a deliberate attempt to exclude her. Why do modern women always rush things? Why can't they just accept things at face value without reading more into things? It's hard to get close to women today. It's like everything has to be choreographed according to plan. I'm just a nice Jewish man who misses his dead wife and the simple life I used to have with her."

"A yellow-bellied, pond scum sucking, no good, lying son-of-a-bitch is what my last girlfriend called me as she was throwing my belongings out into the apartment hallway," said Mike, a twenty-nine year old from Detroit. "She accused me of deceiving her, of pursuing her until I made her weak and dependent and then pulling the rug out from under her. I may be a lot of things but a yellow-bellied, pond scum sucking, no good, lying son-of-a-bitch isn't one of them. Yes, I went crazy over Theresa the minute I set eyes on her. Yes, I couldn't stop thinking about her. And yes, I think I probably fell in love with her that first meeting and would have married her in a heartbeat when we first met. She and I laughed together a lot, but I could tell she was a little less than overly enthusiastic about me. I'm a decent looking guy but no Don Johnson. I asked her out a few times and she kept turning me down saying, that I was a great guy, but she just didn't think I was her type. She finally consented after I sent her a huge card I made that said, TRY ME...YOU'LL LOVE ME.

"We had a good time and I sent her flowers with a card thanking her. I did pursue her, because I was crazy about her. We moved in together about six months later and I was happier than I'd ever been. Suddenly, I went from Mr. Wonderful to a turkey who couldn't even dress himself right. It seemed like weeks after we moved in together, she was criticizing everything. I wanted to make her happy, so I complied with a lot. When she first brought up the subject of marriage about three months later, *I* was the one who hesitated. I simply said, 'I don't know if I want to marry someone who thinks I'm such an idiot all the time.' I didn't say, 'No, it's out of the question.' I simply meant, it's a question I want to think about. Our relationship has some major flaws and unless we can work them out while we're living together, there's no way we will after we're married—"That's when I became the pond scum sucker. Things got so ugly after that, there was no where to go. The saddest thing? I *was* in love with her. I wanted this relationship to work out. I already had seen the faces of our kids in my dreams. Does she honestly think I deliberately set up this master plan to seduce her and then go on to my next victim? I'm a high school gym, teacher not Rudolph Valentino."

"I was dating Pam casually for about three months," said forty year old John, a housing administrator for HUD. When she first brought up the subject of seeing each other exclusively, I knew it was the right thing to do. I really hadn't had much interest in anyone else since I met Pam anyway. I just hadn't thought about it formally before. About two months later she sat me down again and asked me where I saw the relationship headed. Again, I really hadn't given it deep thought. It was a wonderful fulfilling relationship. We had many of the same interests. Pam was an independent woman who had her own life and friends. To me it was turning the corner to something I thought could very well turn into marriage and I told her so. The problem was, she started to get angry and wanted to know specifics. I couldn't give her specifics right then. She told me point blank not to call her again until I could, and that was it. She walked out and I never heard from her again. I called her, and she said unless I was ready to make a commitment to her, she didn't want to see me."

"I don't know," offered Martin, a forty-eight year old patent attorney from Wisconsin. "I think I did screw up my last relationship. I had just come out of a very painful, very costly divorce when I met Eileen. She was everything to me that my ex-wife wasn't. Strong, decisive, outgoing and fun. She'd try new things, and she didn't put so much pressure on me for constant emotional support. After about a year, she started to get edgy, I think, and started talking about our future. I think I just got scared and took off. But now that I think about it, it wasn't anything about Eileen that turned me off, it just was the timing. At that point, I just don't think I was ready for another commitment. I had a series of relationships after her, nothing was as good as that one. I looked her up about two years after we split and she was engaged."

"Every man has a story about the love he lost," said Philip a fifty-seven year old art dealer from San Francisco. "After my divorce, I just wanted a clean break and a fresh start. I sold my insurance agency and moved 3,000 miles across the country. It took me about a year to figure out what I wanted to be when I grew up. Then, one day while in an art gallery, I figured it out. I had always cherished art. I had the money and enough influential friends and contacts to make it work. I opened my own gallery. During that time I met Sandy. She was invaluable to me in helping me set up the business. I couldn't have done it without her, but I think our personal relationship suffered because of the business. Now, in retrospect, I realize that I didn't pay enough attention to her. She just came up on the short end of the stick one too many times. We parted friends and I dove even deeper into work. Now that it's flourishing, I realized I met the right person at the wrong time. She needed a commitment then, and I had already made one—to my business."

"My last girlfriend was always trying to make me feel guilty about spending time with my kids," said Michael a forty-three-year old sales manager for an envelope company. "But after the divorce, I didn't get to see them as often as I wanted to. Once the anger between my ex and me subsided, it was easier to see the kids, and I was making up for lost time. About then I met Jean. She was thirty-five and had no kids. We hit it off pretty quickly and after about four months, moved in together. My kids would call a lot and I wanted them to feel like they could, but it seemed to alienate Jean. When I'd give them extra money to buy sneakers or go to the movies, she'd get resentful and point out how much child support I was already paying my ex. I tried to explain to her that the indulgences wouldn't last forever but since the kids and I we were apart for so many months, this time to bond again was so important. She accused me of putting her second, of not being able to commit to her and our relationship. I had no problem committing, but had she just waited it out, everything would have fallen into place. She moved out just before our ten month anniversary."

" 'I'm getting tired of waiting,' said thirty-three year old Meyer, a security guard for a chemical plant, was how my last girlfriend informed me she wanted a commitment. We had been seeing each other almost a year, but I wasn't ready yet. When I told her that, she got angry and moody... and then she got sarcastic always tossing these barbs about being commitment-phobic my way. Then it became like rebellion. The harder she pushed, the more I withheld, until it just fell apart."

Another reason for much of the confusion over commitment does indeed stem from simple timing—the man we're involved with is not in sync with our timetable or we're not in sync with his. Being in different places at the same time, the issue of commitment is perceived as a push. I compare this to a dog's life and a human's. For every one year of our life, a dog ages about seven. In a relationship, for every one month of a man's involvement, we're two months ahead of him (at least!). It's like, one day Fido is just a puppy tearing up your favorite slippers and before you know it, you're crushing aspirin into his Gravy Train because he's got arthritis in his hip. Well to a man, (not all men mind you, but the majority of men) it's like, one day he's wining and dining his princess, and before he knows it, she's circling strollers in the Spiegel catalog.

Part of the reason is that we're much more open than men, and will divulge more of ourselves more quickly, thus feeling tightly bonded because of it. Men hold back, taking longer to reach the same point.

Think back to a man you dated who rushed things, whether it be going to bed or marriage. You really may have cared for him, but you wanted to *wait* until you felt close to him. His constant pressure started to eat at you. Some of us more verbal types will just say, "ey, you twit, ease up. If you want it, you'll just have to wait until I'm ready to give it to you." Our less verbal sisters will beat around the bush for a while until the pressure gets too much and he backs off or we walk off. The situation is almost identical to one where the relationship has progressed. You want a commitment, and he's the one being reticent. Either way, the predicament becomes a snag when two people who care for each other, arrive at different places at different times. We just handle it so much better when he's taking nine cold showers a day and parts of his anatomy are so blue they could be hung on a Christmas tree as ornaments. *That's because we're in control.*

The part we have a harder time with, is when we perceive that he's not only in control, but reluctant. Reluctant means, "indecisive, unsure, diffident, faltering, halting, hesitant, tentative, waffling, wavering, unwilling, afraid, disinclined, shy, timid" and "uneager" or so says my dictionary. It is not to be construed as: "dead-set against, opposed to" or "anti", as, according to men, most women believe.

SO WHAT HAPPENS NOW?

If you have determined that Mr. Reluctant is someone you want to spend the rest of your life with, and you have a relationship that seems to be headed in that direction, how can you get it over this hump without destroying it and making him into Mr. History?

First, by making sure you don't misread *not now* as *not ever*. Secondly, by keeping in mind that he can be reluctant for many reasons, none of which may mark him as commitment-phobic. By taking a deep breath and the necessary time to find out what objections he really has, you may find that they're easily overcome. The husband of one of my girlfriends didn't propose for almost three years after they started living together. When she was finally brave enough to have a do-or-die type conversation, he got very emotional and told her he had been hoping his retail business would have been doing better, and he wanted to be in a better financial position before they got married. "I wanted us to move right into a house and to be able to afford a proper honeymoon," he said. She settled for a five day cruise and a nice condo. It was Carl she was in love with, not what he could buy her.

Many times a man's private fears about myriad different things, that we wouldn't even think of, get in his way. A frank, nurturing conversation that unearths his objections and answers them, sometimes is all it takes to get most men, who are really in love, over the hump. There are plenty of men (and women too) who think that commitment may impinge on personal freedoms. "Once I'm married, she won't let me... bowl, golf, hanglide or go out with the boys." There are many, many reasons why people view monogamy as the end of autonomy.

But what if he doesn't come up with anything concrete? You must make sure that he feels as emotionally close to you as you feel to him, by building the type of emotional intimacy he responds to. You're already intimate friends, now you have to make him envision the two of you as team players for life—stronger together than apart, and that you'll add to his future not limit it. He needs to be certain he can trust you with his innermost thoughts, and that no matter how angry you become, you'll never use that knowledge against him. He needs to know you love him as is, and that you're not disappointed and constantly looking to change him. He needs to be certain that no matter how bad things get, he can always count on you. He needs to feel accepted, autonomous and appreciated not that you'll turn into his mother and smother him, or a jury who'll hang him.

"I already feel that way about him," you say.

Yes, but is that the message you're clearly sending him? Imagine that you are both buses, destination: Flatbush, in Brooklyn. You're the Express, he's the Local. Starting in Manhattan, you'll both get to the destination... eventually. You're just going to get there first. There you are in Flatbush, tapping your foot, looking at your watch and wondering, *Where the hell could he be?* He started out the same time you did. He had good directions, so you know he can't be lost.

He's not lost, he's delayed!

How do you make sure he'll get there, too?

You follow the suggestions above, you use your own intuition and your knowledge about what makes him happy and what turns him off, and you make sure you become the only woman he can't imagine ever getting there without.

In the progression of most relationships, we follow this yellow brick road pretty well.

We meet someone who attracts us. ("Oooga ooga!")

We begin to discover things we like about him. (Jane swings on a vine. Tarzan swings on a vine.)

True friendship blossoms. ("Jane, you want to swing on my vine?")

The more time we spend with him, the deeper the feeling of trust that develops. If Jane swings on Tarzan's vine, Tarzan will protect her, and not let her fall from the sky like a lead balloon. When we trust someone, we begin to feel close to them. ("Okay, Tarzan, I swing from your vine")

Then we become emotionally attached to them. ("Tarzan?" "Yes, Jane." "I feel happy and safe from those pesky pygmies and their poison darts when I'm with you on your vine.")

They make us feel loved and appreciated. We want to be with them all the time. ("Tarzan?" "Yes, Jane?" "Wouldn't it be great if you and me and a baby boy, making three, swing on vine?")

Now here's where it gets a little touchy. ("Jane?" "Yes, Tarzan?" "I don't think there's room on my vine for baby boy, *just yet.*")

Jane interprets Tarzan's response as noncommittal, red-flag number 121, so she gets antsy. ("Tarzan?" "Yes, Jane?" "Tell me, have other Janes swung on vine?") Bad move Jane, try again.

("Tarzan?" "Yes, Jane?" "You know there are a lot of other big strong Tarzans out there in the jungle, and if ...") Another bad move Jane. Try again.

("Tarzan?" "Yes, Jane?" "You're thirty-nine years old. I'm thirty-six, we can hook up my old vine if we have to. There'll be plenty of room for Boy, Girl and Cheetah, for crying out loud.") Bad, bad move Jane. Give it another go. *Now, Tarzan's getting antsy.*

("Tarzan?" "Yes, Jane?" "If you don't make up your mind soon, I'm getting off this vine. How long do you expect me to sit up here in the sun, with the bugs, and the heat, with the wind and the rain and the humidity and ...")

(Ahhhhhhhhhh Ahhhhhhh.) Tarzan jumped into the Pygmy pit.

The moral of the story is that Jane didn't get it. Had Jane only realized that his answer wasn't, *No way, Jose*, it was, *Not right now*, Jane would not have taken his reluctance personally. It should have sent up a yellow flag, not a red one. Tarzan is driven by logic, Jane by emotion. Jane probably contemplated the commitment question a few hundred times before she even brought the subject up, yet she expected Tarzan to arrive at her conclusion instantly. After all, they've been up there on that vine for some time now. Isn't Tarzan, who is a slave to logic, allowed the same opportunity to arrive at the same conclusion? Isn't it fair to think he'd like to consider the possibility, now that it's on the table, a few hundred times too?

When Jane realized his reluctance she shouldn't have gotten hurt or angry. She should have spent more time becoming an integral part of Tarzan's life. A part he couldn't bear to live without, his best friend and confidant, his partner in love and in life, someone he laughed with, and wasn't afraid to cry with. Someone he knew would never betray his confidences, someone who loved him in spite of the fact he slammed into a tree every now and again and didn't make him feel stupid and scared when he did, someone who was willing to take the time to create the right amount of emotional intimacy that Tarzan must have, in order to arrive at the same mind set.

If Jane had been someone who understood he was reluctant on the subject, not immovable, she might be dancing the Watusi at her $120 a plate, Congo wedding.

Just a note that needs to be interjected here: Just as every man is different, every woman is different and surely every situation is different. There are no universal keys that unlock every door. There are also those men who are professional Mr. Reluctants—men who toy with a woman and who deliberately lie to her. However, these are not the men I address in this book. In *How to Choose Who's Right and Avoid Who's Wrong*, (Chapter 18) there are enough red-flag questions you can ask yourself about him to help you honestly assess if the man you're with is one who is a professional procrastinator or worse. No matter how patient and understanding you are, no matter how much time you give to such a guy, he'll never come around.

"I love you Nanc," John said. "I don't want to ever be without you. I can't even imagine what it would be like living without you," he said, his voice filled with emotion.

"I need to know if there is a solid future. It isn't as if I have rushed you in any way."

"I don't know if we have a future, but we have the present and the present could turn into the future," he said. (?????) That was the day Nancy threw in the towel.

One of my closest friends, Nancy finally walked from a relationship that meant a lot to her, one she nurtured and had high hopes for but knew in her heart, that after almost three years, was never going anywhere. The day she made the decision was a painful day, but the day that ultimately set her free.

You must honestly listen to your own little voice, and if that voice is telling you to be careful, or to read the writing on the wall, don't ignore it. After just a year, you may be jumping the gun pressing for an immediate answer, after three years, your trigger finger had time to atrophy. A man, even a non-committal one, who's bringing you presents or who professes his love, is comforting and hard to resist. It's orgasmic and we get drunk from its effect. We not only ignore our little voice when we're in this situation, we sometimes turn the volume off completely. That's why we get hurt, and why many decent, deserving men take the rap for the creeps. Not all men are creeps, and the vast majority of men are not commitment phobic. But even so, sometimes you can do everything right and you still may just be the wrong cover for his pot. You have to know when to hold them, and when to fold them. You can lead a horse to water but you cannot make him drink. A zillion cliches fit here, none of them comforting. Walking away is never easy, especially when you have time and a great deal of emotion invested. Nancy was afraid to let go of something she loved. She was afraid of being lonely, but she healed in time, and found someone else.

What I offer you here, is what men have told me—that the relationships that go the distance are the ones where closeness bonds two people as one. Even though you may love someone, you have to respect that the bonding process develops quickly for some and more slowly for others. Stop feeling as though men are saying *No*; recognize they might just be saying *No, not now*. Instead, before you goad, address his feelings about closeness, commitment and change. Ask yourself if his reticence could have anything to do with your behavior towards him? Were you initially attracted to something that made him seem invincible and desirable, but now that you know him, he's nothing more than a mere mortal? Did he really change, or is it just your perception of him that's altered? Are you discounting his non-verbal attempts at showing you love, and demonstrating your anger in ways that make him hold back? Do you really love this person enough to work at jumping the hurdles? If you do, just make sure you don't drive someone away who's only crime was his unpreparedness for the test.

Part Five
How To Mature With A Man

Chapter 19

He Said, She Thought -
The Secrets For Compassionate Communication Between The Sexes

If love makes the world go round, then communication clearly propels it. The only problem is that communication's evil twin, misunderstanding, rears its ugly head every so often, further mucking up the loving process.

If the subject of commitment elicits such passionate responses from men and women, the topic of communication between the sexes makes the little veins on everyone's neck pop out.

"She never stops talking."

"He just doesn't open up and share his feelings."

"She doesn't ever understand what I mean, so why bother talking?"

"He only gets angry when I want to talk."

"She analyzes everything to death. You can't have a conversation. It turns into a science experiment."

"He can't stand it when I give him advice."

"She turns every conversation into a battle."

"I feel like I'm walking on eggshells when I talk to her. I have to say just the right thing or I'm branded insensitive."

"He invalidates how I feel."

"She doesn't talk—she vents."

The number one response given by a whopping 77% of the 4,000 American women surveyed in 1987 by Shere Hite when asked, "What does your partner do that makes you the maddest?"—"He never listens to me." *Oy, vay is that a hot bed of contention!*

Why do we feel so isolated by our attempts to talk to someone we love? One theory popularized by the success of Deborah Tannen's, *You Just Don't Understand,* is that men and women "speak different languages," and although Tannen adroitly addresses many of the reasons men and women misunderstand each other, many among us prefer the *different language* theory—a seductive excuse allowing both men and women to avoid any responsibility for the breakdown in communication. But according to Suzette Haden Elgin, Ph.D., in her book *Genderspeak,* men and women do *not* have inherently different language styles. She suggests that "male/female communication does not have to be either armed combat or endless mystifying tedium. It does not have to be the source of either rage or misery. It can and should be effective, efficient, and a source of mutual satisfaction."

Easier said than done, right? We say there is no magic wand or a universal key that can unlock the mystery of creating a long-term successful relationship, but I think there is. I believe it starts by learning *how* to speak to each other and then taking the time to understand what our partner actually means by his or her words, *before we react.*

When I was younger, I was a much more reactive person than I am now. In retrospect, I admit I had a harder time then making friends, keeping friends and just generally being understood – by either sex. Then, a wonderful thing happened in my thirties. Along with my two gray hairs, a lovely assortment of what the dermatologist affectionately labeled "skin tags," and an exceptionally deep wrinkle under my right eye, came a calmness and introspection and what I guess could be called an *attitude adjustment.* Suddenly, the things that would cause me to react abruptly didn't anymore. The senseless misunderstandings that had plagued so much of my life virtually disappeared.

What happened? Did God come down from the heavens and hand me the tablet containing the missing link in my communication skills? Did I enter the hospital for a simple tonsillectomy and did they perform a partial lobotomy as a two-for-one bonus? Not quite, but my mother seems to thinks so. What happened was that I almost lost one of my best friends over what now seems like a ridiculous disagreement. I thought she said something to hurt me and although she did utter certain words, she meant something entirely different than what I heard. Instead of reacting as I had previously, which was to get angry and escalate the conflict, I mustered my self-esteem and simply asked her if she meant to hurt my feelings. For what seemed like an eternity, she looked at me as if I were a Martian from another planet. "Of course not, you twit," she said. "I love you and would never intentionally do anything to hurt you," going on to explain what she really meant by her words, which had little in common with my interpretation. It was then that it dawned on me, why the outcome of this situation ended so satisfactorily for me, and why so many identical situations hadn't.

It was me. My reaction was different.

Why? Because so seldom in my life had I felt close enough to someone to *allow myself* to be vulnerable to them, vulnerable enough to turn the other cheek, so to speak. Vulnerable enough to say the words, "I'm hurt and confused." This was one of the few relationships in my life that was important enough to hang on to. Important enough to drop the suit of armor which has always protected me. Usually, if I were hurt or angry, I would pick up my marbles and retreat, or I'd intensify the situation by trying to wound them as they had wounded me. Either way, I remained hurt and no more sapient. How many of us can accurately tell the difference between innocent miscommunication or willful ones? It suddenly occurred to me how often in our relationships we react out of hurt predicated on misunderstanding rather than fact. How many times does a seemingly insignificant conversation end in argument with our partner hurt, angry and feeling very, very lonely in one room and us feeling the same way in another room? Perhaps far more often than any of us care to admit.

Being the information hound that I am, I read a great many

books on the subject of language, and I started to listen. If I didn't think I understood something, I simply asked for clarification. Suddenly a whole world opened for me when I stopped reacting and started *listening*. Applying this new-found knowledge to my life brought tens of deep, warm relationships that have endured a decade or more. My friendships with men and women crystallized to such extents, I continually feel blessed. It's not to say that I don't get stressed out or have arguments any more; I certainly do. It's just that now the outcome doesn't dissipate the strength of the relationship... or cause its demise. People compliment me again and again on my compassion, on my ability to see both sides. I always knew it was there, I just wasn't expressing it adequately enough for anyone else to recognize it. Now it's *a part* of my personality people say they're drawn to. Certainly, if the original *rebel without a cause* can do it, anyone can, if they care to.

I wanted to know why some people seemed to *get along* with others effortlessly while others seem to always have a hard time of it. What have I learned? *It's the way they communicate how they feel, and the way they compute the messages they receive.*

I think this is especially significant in relationships between the sexes. When people don't understand how to communicate with each other properly or how to argue constructively, the hurt and anger magnifies over time, eradicating the love, respect and emotion we feel for each other. The insidious thing about unresolved conflict is, it strips away a teeny, tiny piece of each of us every time it happens. Left unchecked, the relationship invariably disintegrates. We have all been exposed to relationships that seemed to improve and thrive over time—deepening and growing within couples who have been married ten, twenty or thirty years and are still playful and in-love with each other. All too often we've also seen other relationships that after only three or four years become vapid, shallow, barren unions that ignite only in battle.

We surely don't start out like this. We launch our relationships in love and with high hopes for the future, but we let them erode over time. We *let* them deteriorate because we adopt the position that good relationships *just happen*. The prospect of having to continually work at relationships seems like an added burden—a burden that's in direct conflict with the *love's-the-answer* philosophy so many of us prefer. The good news is that it's not back-breaking work. The bad news is, love alone isn't enough. The salient factor remains, that in order to have sustained happiness in a relationship you must have compassionate communication. You must have mutual respect. It's simply learning to treat our partner with more compassion and tenderness as time goes on, not just at the beginning.

This is a good place to go back and reread chapters twelve and thirteen—*The "Why Factor"* and *Determining Lifestyle Compatibility*.

Why does it seem we have such a hard time talking to and understanding each other? Women insist that men are uncommunicative, and men insist that women are overly analytical. Since this book is devoted to the way men think, in this chapter I have isolated many of the common communication conflicts that men have told me breakdown their love for a woman, and offer strategies that can help strengthen the bonds rather than weaken them. Strategies that, if incorporated early on in a relationship, can insure a union that strengthens and grows and can withstand any storm—emotional or otherwise. We *can* make our love last; we *can* make the passion endure. But, in order to do that, we must first commit to *non-reactive* understanding of how we each communicate with the other and what those communications really mean.

COMMUNICATION BREAKDOWN #1

"I can't get no respect". She said, "Why can't you just..." He thought, *She talks to me as if I'm an idiot*.

"When we first met," commented Ryan, a forty-two year old propane gas company executive from Pennsylvania,"she complimented me on almost everything. Now a year later, I don't seem to be able to do anything right. She'll look at me first thing in the morning and say, 'You're not going to wear that tie with that shirt, are you?' I get so angry, I wear it just out of spite. If I have it on, she knows darn well that I intended to wear it. If she doesn't like the tie, why can't she just soften how she indicates that."

<u>Try</u> <u>A</u> <u>Little</u> <u>Tenderness</u>. Sometimes, after we have been in a relationship for a while, we become so familiar with our partner that we forget to show each other respect—the same respect we readily offer veritable strangers. Sometimes the way we speak to our partner mirrors some anger we're harboring from a past, unresolved argument. That's very destructive, for it sets up a chain reaction of hostility and resentment that can poison days, weeks and even the rest of our love life. Years ago, common pleasantries were the rule, not the exception. "Good Morning!" and "How are you?" were daily occurrences. Say that in Manhattan tomorrow and someone will likely fire a warning shot over your head. "Please" and "Thank you" are words we teach our children so that they may become well mannered adults, yet we rarely say these words to our partners. For example, by simply altering the combative statement above to, 'Good morning, honey. Wow, don't you look great today, except that tie just doesn't seem to fit'. You're getting your point across without trashing his self-esteem in the process. Men say they are especially confused, if our gripe doesn't make sense to them, or if they don't attach the same significance to it that we do. When the words we use deflate a man's ego, he will simply detach. If you care enough to be in a relationship with someone, isn't it worth a bit of extra effort to insure that it stays healthy and happy? Even today, when I am the recipient of less-than-subtle criticism, I bristle like a porcupine with her quills on edge. Even though your suggestion may be right on the mark, deliver it so he feels complimented and not like the breath was kicked out of him, is the surest way to bond him to you. He'll think, "This is a woman I can trust. She won't make me feel stupid, even when she can."

Communication Breakdown #2

<u>The</u> <u>Turtle</u> <u>Syndrome</u>. She said, "He doesn't share his feelings and withdraws." He thought, *Why bother? She turns every conversation into a monologue about what's wrong with me.*

Just as in the previous scenario, most men have egos that are more fragile than we may expect. They are physically stronger, so we assume that since they are quieter by nature, it must mean they are the strong silent type. This isn't always the case. They are deeply hurt by our words; they just don't display hurt as readily as we do. "I was very much in love with my ex-fiancee," said Nathan, a twenty-seven year old luxury auto mechanic. "I knew she came from a monied family. She had a lot of class and knowledge about the finer things. Things I wasn't exposed to. Hell, her family *owned* the kinds of cars I just *worked* on. When she introduced me to fine wines, to certain books and art, I was very grateful and I absorbed it all like a sponge. But then, she started correcting everything I did and everything I said. I'm not an ill-mannered slob, I simply didn't have the luxury of money. She began to make me doubt myself in too many ways. I had to leave."

Constructive criticism of our partner is evidence of loving them. Constant criticism is the fastest way to make a man withdraw. Men have stated over and over again that when a woman continuously points out flaw after flaw, it makes him not just angry at her for acting like his mother, but angry at himself for being so imperfect. And that causes him to isolate, what I call, acting like a *turtle*. There he is, Mr. Turtle, be-bopping along at a snail's pace minding his own business, when up ahead he sees that yappy Yorkshire Terrier from the neighborhood. He tries to change direction, but she spots him and makes a beeline for him. One too many yaps and Mr. Turtle yanks all his parts back into the shell and that Yorkie can yap all she wants; he's not coming out until he wants to. Generally, that's when she gets tired of yapping, and leaves.

Men act like a turtle constantly, and we read that as *insensitivity* and deem him callous or cold, when, in actuality, he's hurt, or just confused. Even if you have to bite the bullet, the first few times you deliver your grievance by *sugar-coating* your words, watch how the extra effort you're putting into your love floods back to you. However, if you've been speaking sharply to your partner, you may have to wait until he realizes that your gestures are genuine. He may pop back into that shell although you've said or done nothing to cause it. He may need some time to be sure there's no minefield he's unwittingly being led through. Simply changing your tone and softening your words can and will keep your relationship from withering and dying. It will actually bring you closer and deepen the devotion and trust between you. Respect is the secret ingredient endemic to couples who stay in love.

COMMUNICATION BREAKDOWN #3

Hear No Evil, See No Evil, Speak No... Nothing? She said, "He never talks to me." He thought, *I would, but you just don't seem to like what I have to say.*

"If you don't give me something to work with," I told an applicant, "I don't think I can really write a profile that will do you justice. What are you looking for in a woman?" I persisted.

"Someone who's kind and accepting," he answered.

"What do you mean by accepting?"

"Just a woman who will let me be me."

"What kind of man are you," I asked, thinking I'll come back to the woman question later.

"A nice guy."

And so it went. To me, it was like pulling teeth. I had spent a good forty minutes just trying to get this guy to open up, even a little. With barely a few scribbled sentences in my notebook, it was clear that as patient and reassuring as I was trying to be, I wasn't getting anywhere. "Clyde," I said, "my gut tells me you are a good man, a really good guy. You're obviously sensitive, (which made him blush) you're soft-spoken and I believe with all my heart that you're empathetic and caring, but you're not giving me anything to go on. I can't get anything concrete to convey to our readers. Perhaps you're just a bit too shy for the magazine. Maybe this isn't a good choice for you."

With a tight smile straining his handsome features, thirty-six year old Clyde, a fourth generation Mississippi farmer, poured out what seemed like a lifetime of hurt and confusion. "I'm the quiet type," he stated meekly. "I don't have a lot to say, but when I do, I say it. I was raised that way. It seemed my dad hardly talked to my mom, and she made *me* suffer because of it. She'd gather the family for dinner, hoping for some 'family conversation.' Dad sat there mostly in silence, except for what I called his conceptual grunts. They were always fighting.

"When I married, it was to a small town girl with big city tastes. We disagreed about a lot of things, and she'd accuse me of being small-minded and never wanting to amount to anything or to go places. I *was* amounting to something, and I was going somewhere; it was just different from the direction *she wanted* me to go. When I took the time to weigh things in my mind rather than just react, she'd get angry and tell me I didn't care. When it got to be too much, I'd just shut down. Then she accused me of being closed, just like my father. But I *was* talking. With her I was talking. I consciously made the decision to become something different from my father, but you know what happened?", he asked more to himself than to me, his deep blue-eyes ablaze with emotion. "She just didn't like what I had to say. She'd tell me I was insensitive and cold, unemotional and thick. I'm not any of those things, but when I tried to tell her how I felt about something, if it wasn't in agreement with her thoughts *exactly*, she'd attack me, or cry. I didn't know what to do. Do you have any idea how that made me feel? Even when I'd say, 'I love you, I want to work it out. I just don't agree with you.' She'd say 'You couldn't love me and act this way.' But I did love her, I just didn't accept her point of view. But it wasn't ever that I didn't want to compromise. I would have done anything for us to be happy, but the more I tried, the more she'd belittle me or accuse me of not caring. The more she told me I was distant, the more distant I became.

Eventually, I disappeared from the marriage altogether—just like my father, who I spent half my life hating because I thought he was just cold and self-absorbed.

"My dad's dead now. You know, I never got to ask him if this is how he *was made* to feel. I thought he was *born* like that.

"What do I want in a woman?" he asked again, more to himself than to me. "I want to love a woman who can love me just for who I am. I'm not some fancy banker. I'm a farmer who leads a good, clean life. I don't run around. I don't drink. I'm a good guy who'd be a great father and a great husband if I could find a woman who'd just accept me. I'm not perfect. I have flaws, but I'm reasonable. I believe in compromise. Why does a woman feel the need to be hypercritical if you're simply disagreeing with her. It doesn't mean I don't love her. I want a woman who understands that. That's the kind of woman I can be in love with forever."

The interview lasted almost three hours longer than normal. Clyde turned out to be one of the kindest, sweetest, most sensitive man I'd ever met—an uncomplicated country man with infinite wisdom, *afraid* to talk, not *unwilling* to.

<u>See the Relationship Through His Eyes</u>. As women we have the ability to control our relationships with men. I can hear the scream of dissension now—men are so controlling and so moody, how is *our* control possible? Most men are happiest and healthiest in a relationship and deep down they know it. They need us and they want us, not just because we can find their keys and know where their socks are, but because a loving, fulfilling relationship brings about well being and a sense of belonging and happiness. Everyone wants to be loved. No one enters a relationship looking to demean the other, but all too often we allow our conflicts to escalate to out and out war. This constant struggle for power keeps both of us unbalanced and feeling lost and dejected, alienated from the very person we need to feel the closest to.

The fact that men need us and they know it, sometimes puts us at odds with them. Because of that, we have the ability to bring out the best in them or *the worst*. How we can use that information to our best advantage is all in how we approach men. Asking him to tell you honestly what he feels and thinks about the relationship and listening to him without becoming angry or defensive is a start. Ask him what you do that makes him the angriest or the most uncomfortable. Make sure he knows that you want to listen and that no matter how honest he is you'll be objective, *not critical*. (You can have an honest exchange and give him the same information as long as each criticism is handled calmly without emotion, as if you are both strategically tackling a complicated work problem). Doing this in small stages over insignificant things, allows him to build up the trust that is essential for emotional intimacy. Trust, that when he offers his opinion, he won't be negatively judged for his thoughts. It's only when he's afraid of unfavorable reaction is he unwilling to talk. Most men *will gladly* talk if the conversation doesn't cause them to feel guilty or heap blame on them for all that's wrong with the relationship.

I am not suggesting you have to agree with him or even accept his point of view. You certainly don't. But if you want to love him *long term* and have him communicate with you openly, you must be able to have calm, nurturing, discussions where both parties feel comfortable and able to freely exchange opinions, whether you agree or not. A note: we may not judge the men in our lives as harshly as some perceive we do. The fact that they *feel* we're judging them so harshly, is why this point was worthy of addressing.

COMMUNICATION BREAKDOWN #4

Making a connection. She said, "Why can't he just sit down and discuss his day with me when he comes home. It would make us closer." He thought, *"I'm mentally exhausted. Why can't we just sit and unwind?"*

"The minute I walk through the door, she wants to have a meaningful exchange," said Gary, a forty-seven year old pharmacist. "She gives me a blow-by-blow of her day, which I do my best to listen to, and then she wants the same from me. I'm exhausted from my day. I listen to problems all day long and then she dumps on me and wants me to have this bonding conversation. I'm lucky I can even focus both eyes in the same direction. Then she gets angry or hurt and weepy, and we spend half the night not even speaking to each other, which she accuses me of masterminding all along."

<u>Put</u> <u>Yourself</u> <u>in</u> <u>Your</u> <u>Partner's</u> <u>Place</u>. As we discussed in the last chapter, women seem to function best with a daily dose of *verbal* closeness, which is not as important to most men. They value the closeness, just not the *verbal* route of getting there. Even though both partners may come home equally tired, she wants to share her thoughts, which helps her unwind; he just wants to vegetate his way of doing the same. Some couples go through this impasse in the morning or on lazy weekends. She pops out of bed wanting to solve the problem of world hunger, and he just wants to get his toothbrush in his mouth without poking out one of his eyes (Or vice versa). Nothing is wrong with either one, they're just different. It goes back to the way we've been socialized—women, by getting everything off our chests; men, by sort of decompressing... slowly. This becomes confrontational when women, frustrated by this, view it as a form of rejection and act accordingly, when in fact, it's far from rejection. Men have said over and over that they want to be loving and intimate with their partner, especially after a hard day. "The last thing I want is for us to end up in different rooms, angry at each other," Gary said. "I want to be able to reach out and touch her; it's just that I can't accomplish that by talking. I'm practically brain-dead when I come home. I just want quiet."

This impasse can be handled in a positive way by both parties honestly discussing their conversational needs with each other... preferably at a time when both are equally rested and ready for the discussion. If you understand he's not rejecting you, the time can be used to take a relaxing bath, stopping at the department store, or if you really need to blow off steam, phoning a friend. Women would do best not to be conversationally monogamous. If you want him to meet your needs, ask him to set a prearranged time with you. Nothing mandated, just some neutral time where *you* can get the interaction you need to catch up, communicate and feel close. By setting aside maybe twenty minutes or so after the news, or during breakfast, both partners can get what they need without alienating the other.

We have to remember that men just aren't as verbal as we are. They cherish the companionability of just being together. They don't need or reap the same release that we derive from verbal exchanges, and we must respect that. A man who says "I'm not in the mood to talk right now." or "I just want to sit and read the paper for a while." is not rejecting you. He's honestly telling you how *he* feels.

Instead of becoming hurt and resentful, just try saying, "That's Okay, but I have something I would like to discuss with you, could we talk before we go to work tomorrow?" Most men will appreciate your understanding and will gladly meet you halfway. Showing a man that you care enough for him to place some of *his* needs before yours will instill in him the desire to do the same. However, a man who will never set aside some time to talk or one who's totally preoccupied when he does *consent* to talk, looking around you at the TV for example, is selfish, and he's a self-centered person who will never meet your needs, since he's too busy meeting his own. Once you've given that kind of man the benefit of the doubt several times by calmly conveying your desire and need to talk, and he still won't, *dump him*. I know it's easier said than done, but he's the kind of man who will never grow with you. He'll live parallel to you. And even a zillion friends can't compensate for that kind of emptiness.

COMMUNICATION BREAKDOWN #5

Mixed Messages. She said, "He says one thing, then does another." He thought, *I say one thing and do another?! Women wrote the book on it!!*

We've all heard the classic story of the woman who tells her beloved, that since money has been tight she doesn't want an anniversary present. "Honey, our anniversary is next month and I've been thinking, let's save what we would have spent on presents for something more important." He agrees. The day of the anniversary arrives and she wakes him up to find a present and a card on his chest. "Happy anniversary!" she exclaims.

He's dumbfounded and doesn't know what to do or say. Did he buy her a present? No. Why? Because she told him not to. She cries or is depressed and doubting his love for her the rest of the day, or week. "I didn't think he'd listen to me," she complains to her sister. "I thought he still could have gone out and gotten me a card or flowers." Expressing her hurt, she's cool to him on the one special day they've both been looking forward to.

He's hurt and confused too, although we don't recognize it or don't rank his hurt on a par with ours.

"Go to work," my friend Elaine told her boyfriend while rubbing her multi-colored ankle. "I'll be fine. See, it doesn't even look like a basketball anymore, it's settled nicely into sort of a smaller, football shape; the swelling is going down; I'll be fine. There's no reason the two of us have to be cooped up here —isolated from the world and humanity, lonely and maimed. Go. Go to work, do what you need to do; I'll be fine."

He went. She called me eighteen minutes later to tell me what an insensitive beast he was. "How could he not know how much I needed him and wanted him to stay?"

"Elaine," I said. "The man is a computer analyst. He's used to getting little direct messages on a screen two feet from his face that tell him what to do. He's not good at guessing. If you wanted him to stay, you should have said so."

"I wanted him to know; I wanted him to stay."

She wanted him to read her mind.

From my conversations with both men and women, it is clear that mixed messages add to the communication dilemma. Very often, since we are such intuitive creatures, we believe that because we can read what others really think and separate it from what they say, that our men are equally adept at this. It baffles them!! They look at us like we should have satin turbans and talk like gypsy... *eyn short, littal frayses.* To most men, our ability to predict what someone means is astounding. They take facts and make sound guesstimates. We take minor innuendo and come up with solid fact.

The only way around this is to be clearer, although clarifying every situation is not always as practical in love as it is in the office. "So Mr. Thompson, I will expect the proposal from your company to be on my desk by next Thursday morning," is much easier said than "So Tom, I would like a card and chocolates on our anniversary even though I told you I *vanted nating. If ve say ve vant nating and ve get nating, ve got vat ve asked for. If ve vant sumting - ve need to zay zo.*

This is an area in which women would fair better and be hurt less if we were able to convey our wishes and feelings in a clear cut manner. We just have to accept the fact that the majority of men are lousy prognosticators. If we want them to know how we feel, we either have to tell them, or hand over our magic turban.

COMMUNICATION BREAKDOWN #6

Verbal Support. She said, "When I tell him about my plans or dreams, he's such a downer." He thought, *She doesn't give me a chance to be supportive. If I want to stop and consider what she said, she takes that as a put-down.*

"My last girlfriend came to me one night, and out of the blue started talking about setting up a video store," said thirty-nine year old Kent from New Haven, Connecticut. "She said she had read an ad in the paper that said we could open our own for a $15,000 investment. She had already predicted we'd triple our investment in a year. When I said I didn't think it could possibly be that easy, she told me I was a downer who always squelched her ideas. All I wanted to do was think about it, and carefully assess it. Am I always supposed to be a cheerleader even if I see problems?"

All of us have a need to feel understood and appreciated. When we express an idea to our man, we want him to share in the enthusiasm of the moment. Women tend to work things out as they go along, sometimes discussing idea after idea with no real intention of employing any of them until she thinks about it further herself. The communication dilemma is that men don't always understand that. Since they are logic driven, they want to consider all the realities before even imagining such a possibility. A man's inclination is to focus on the negative side of any new situation. He's really not being critical at all, he just goes through the evaluation process differently. By patiently listening to what he says, he'll respect and admire your clear, cool head and relate to you better. In my own relationship, I withhold the dreamy part of my ideas from my husband until I have formulated a realistic plan of my own. Then after I share it with him, I carefully listen to how he feels, and if he doesn't jump up and down, I don't take it personally, anymore. His logic has saved my visionary behind countless times.

COMMUNICATION BREAKDOWN #7

Expressing our needs. She said, "If he loves me, he'll just know how I feel." He Thought, *What does she expect me to be, a mindreader?*

"I hate to shop," said Jim a fifty-seven year old carpenter, "and Jean knows it, so instead of asking me, she hints or tells me about the wonderful guys she sees walking hand in hand with their women in the malls. Sometimes I pick up on it and will go with her, just to shut her up. Other times I just don't understand, and then she gets angry. Sometimes it's days until I figure out why she's being so hostile. I hate to shop, but I certainly don't mind going with her every once in a while, but she wants me to guess what she wants."

This is sort of a broader view of the mixed message dilemma. Women were socialized differently than men. Girls never bragged about their accomplishments, whereas men were given greater latitude in this area. Men requested what they wanted.

Women didn't ask directly for what they wanted, for fear they'd be deemed aggressive and demanding. Many of us have overcome that archaic fear and understand that expressing our needs will not be considered aggressive behavior except by the most dimwitted of all Neanderthals. Again, it's all in the approach. A laundry list of wants, spewed in succession, is surely a turn off. However, the vast majority of men say a far bigger turn off is having to guess. "There is nothing that makes me crazier than having to guess what my girlfriend wants. The fact that I'm just not capable of doing it infuriates me. Her hostility when I can't do it, just shuts me down. I turn off to her because I think it's so unfair and such an unrealistic expectation of any man," said Kirk a thirty-three year old firefighter from Austin, Texas.

Most men feel completely helpless when a woman *hints* at what she wants simply because the majority of men don't ever have the foggiest idea of what we mean. The way to keep fluent in our communications with our partners is for us to simply *ask* when we have a need. We don't have to demand, but there's nothing harmful, demeaning, or embarrassing, in stating a desire. Most men say that setting aside time for a "meeting each others needs" conversation, where each partner knows what's on the agenda, would be extremely worthwhile. But that's not a time to criticize, "I'm not happy because you never spend enough time with me on the weekends," but rather, it's a time to express needs constructively. "On the weekends, it's important to me to spend a little more time with you." Most men say that when a suggestion is made to them in a kind way, or in such a way that they aren't made to feel that they are solely responsible, they aren't immediately on the defensive the way they would be when the information is delivered as a criticism. They also say that unless the request is unreasonably outlandish, they not only will meet most of our needs, but they'll appreciate not having to figure them out or suffer the consequences if they don't. "I finally asked Jean to simply *ask* me when she wanted me to shop with her instead of hinting. Now she does, and I don't mind going with her more often. Maybe I was just rebelling from the *way* she requested my company. I still don't like to shop, but I love her and know how much she enjoys us doing it together. Considering my feelings by asking me, doesn't put the same pressure on me anymore, and it seems is easier. I may not always be able or even *want* to meet all her needs, but I finally made her realize her *having* needs isn't what infuriated me, having to guess at what they were was what started the conflicts."

COMMUNICATION BREAKDOWN #8

<u>Consider, Don't Comment</u>. She said, "He can't ever take advice. He gets angry and explodes." He thought, *Why can't she just listen instead of giving me her advice. She always invalidates my feelings and antagonizes me when all I'm looking for is a little consolation.*

"When I told her my house had been robbed," said Myron, a fifty-two year old furniture chain CEO, she gave me one security idea after another. Keyless locks, extra deadbolts, security system monitors. I had forgotten to activate my alarm system before I went out. I knew it was partly because of my negligence. All I wanted her to do was listen. I didn't understand why I got so angry at her. She said I was taking my frustration out on her. We had a terrible fight and she went home to her apartment feeling awful, and I was left in my messy house feeling hurt, angry and very alone. It wasn't until I spoke with a couple I met at the office of my insurance agency that I realized why I got so angry at my fiancee. Their home had also been robbed. When the couple and I spoke, they told me how frustrated and violated they felt. They said they almost were afraid to sleep in their house. The woman said she actually grieved for the loss of her jewelry, not because of its monetary value, but because some of the pieces were from her mother and grandmother and were irreplaceable. 'I wanted to hand those pins down to my daughter and my granddaughter.' It was then I realized that's just how I felt. I didn't care that my watches and rings were taken, but one watch belonged to my father; it was the only thing of value he had and I wanted to give it to my son. The couple validated how I felt. We just listened to each other."

As women, we all have a tendency to want to make things better. By offering our opinions or comments, its our way of trying to mend the situation, but very often men just want your ear. They want us to say, "You must feel awful. I understand. I just want you to know I'm here for you." No comments, no solutions, no advice; it's a matter of just being able to listen attentively.

I remember, after my miscarriage in the third year of my marriage, the hordes of well-meaning friends who fed me one horror story after another of those even more unfortunate than me. Or worse, the people who told me it was meant to be or that the child would have been abnormal had it been born. I loved everyone who cared enough to try to make me feel better. My mother shared my feeling because she had lost a child, too. But my husband was the only one who understood how I felt just then; everyone consoled me and lost sight of the fact that it was his child too, and it was *our* loss.

Responding to what I call negative situations: the loss of a job, an important project, a traffic ticket, a bad day, an illness, etc., by offering even the most heartfelt, well-meaning advice ,sometimes can cause the person we're offering it to, to feel that his feelings (or hers, for that matter) are not being understood. And just a note: There are those that pull into themselves (turtle) when something bad happens. They are not rejecting you. These are people that do best when they are left alone. A simple touch accompanied by "I want to be here for you. I want to comfort you, but I don't know how," is sometimes all they need, to know you care and that their feelings matter. If you offer and they still say they'd rather be alone, respect that. Some people need quiet time to emerge from a blue-funk.

COMMUNICATION BREAKDOWN #9

<u>Make up your mind</u>. She said, "He never has an opinion

about what we should do or even what kind of food to eat." He thought, *The minute I do, she says it's not what she was in the mood for.*

I fall victim to this myself. "What do you want for dinner?" I ask my husband on the four or so nights a week we eat out or order in. "I don't care," comes the standard answer which is followed by the standard, "Whatever you want." I chirp back, "You make the decision. Anything's Okay with me." Silence for about three minutes and fifteen seconds before he says, "How 'bout wings?" Nine seconds to realize, *Wings... yuck.* "No. I'm in the mood for Chinese," I say. Dead silence while he fumes and silently thinks, *Why didn't you just say that in the first place?*

And why didn't I? Well, nothing was really in my mind until he said wings. Then it was clear that wings was not what I felt like. Suddenly, Chinese was. We don't do this to intentionally infuriate men, although the majority of men do list this under their top twenty pet peeves. On a small scale this is harmless. Done continuously, it creates animosity and resentment and is the cause of him clamming up. "My girlfriend is always begging me to go shopping with her. I like to shop, just not with her" said thirty-nine year old Don, heir to a Pittsburgh electronics firm. She'll say, 'Help me pick out a birthday present for my Dad,' and I'm willing to, but everything I suggest, she rejects."

"My fiancee was running late the Sunday we planned a picnic with her son and my two daughters, so she called and asked if I could run to the store and pick up the supplies. I asked her what kind of cold-cuts she wanted me to get. She said it didn't matter. 'Just get what you like,' she said. So, I did. The entire picnic she complained that I didn't get the right stuff. 'Kevin doesn't eat salami and roast beef,' she said. She never told me that. I told her I'd never go shopping for her again unless she gave me a specific list. That made her mad. The picnic was ruined for both of us, but the kids had a great time. They ate pickles, candy and potato chips... the stuff I like."

Men say they have opinions about everything—the kinds

of clothes we wear, the kinds of food they like to eat, the kinds of presents we should buy. They have as many opinions as we do, in most cases. They say the problem is that women reject their suggestions so routinely, they just don't bother anymore. "She already knows what she wants," said Elliott, a twenty-nine year old eyewear salesman. "Why does she even waste the energy asking me?"

As I've said before in this book, women tend to think out loud. The opinions of others helped to solidify or modify our own ideas. Women certainly don't mean to torture their mates by rejecting their ideas all the time. So how do you get past this communication block? By validating his suggestion by considering it. "You know, I think Dad would love the do-it-yourself gun rack for the back of his Mercedes, but I remember him saying he could really use new slippers. If I can't find the slippers, the gun-rack would be great." Again, it takes a second to shoot your mate's self-esteem through with holes. It may just take a few added seconds to make sure he feels appreciated. When he's appreciated, he's happier and healthier, and he stays more available to you emotionally, and he'll be more forthcoming with ideas.

Chapter 20 | Romance – What It Is And What It Is Not

WHAT IT IS

When questioned about being romantic, an enthusiastic 97% of the men queried emphatically said, "Yes," they considered themselves anywhere from moderately romantic to *"very"* romantic.

When women were asked the same set of questions a full 100% responded with an unequivocal, "yes," with the vast majority considering themselves "extremely romantic." Many women even qualified their answer with an illustration of their romantic creativity. That's a curious thing. If 99% of the men and a resounding 100% of the women interviewed claim they are true romantics... why are there so many people who *crave* romance from their partner? What's going on in relationships?

We fantasize about romance, we thirst for it, yet most people feel it's the essential element *missing* in their lives. Romance is an ideal. True romance is a state of mind. It's an ebullient feeling of being *one* with another. Everyone who's in love, experiences the intoxicating rush of romance. Suddenly almost any situation can become a romantic encounter. We stop at card stores unprovoked and spend hours reading card after card, until we select just the right one, or a series of right ones. Just the exercise itself is romantic. How will he react when he reads it? Will he smile? What will he think? Will it fill him with emotion?

We hypothesize in our heads, and even the supposing brings us pleasure. We plan a special dinner, a spur-of-the-moment picnic, a breakfast-in-bed or we stuff a surprise in a packed lunch. We buy a shirt he's been eying, a book he's mentioned or tickets to watch his favorite team play. Romance is a phone call just to say, "I was thinking of you." It's a special touch, the nibbling of his ear or your tongue lightly grazing his finger while you gaze into his eyes. Romance is an electrical current that invisibly and inextricably connects two people; a current activated by a simple word, the smell of his cologne on your pillow, the meeting of your eyes or the touch of his hot breath. The pulchritude of romance is powerfully magnetic for it coils our hopes, our dreams and our sense of worth around our lover.

Like a moth to a flame, many are addicted to the ecstasy of romantic love and blindly go from relationship to relationship in search of the fix that will revive the feeling, mainlining the euphoria, reveling in the rapture and bewildering when it's gone. Others sadly accept its retreat, and live in the shadows with memories of what was and what could have been.

How can we possibly be content to live this way? Wouldn't it be simpler and hurt less to learn how to sustain our love? With all the information and technological advancements of today, how is it possible we still adhere to the antiquated paradigm that romance just *occurs?*

If you don't eat, won't your body deteriorate and perish?

If you don't water your plants, won't they wither and die?

If you don't put gas in your car won't it cease to run?

Then why do we believe romance has the power to invigorate *itself?* Doesn't the desire for romance need to be nurtured and tended the same way we fortify and nourish anything we care for?

Of course the answer is yes. But it certainly is not the popular answer, for it centers added responsibility for the *outcome* of relationships squarely upon our already overburdened shoulders.

"When the woman I'm involved with goes out of her way to show me she was thinking of me," said a handsome thirty-six year old flight attendant from North Carolina, "I feel special, I feel confident and I believe she's telling me something important, something that means she desires, wants, and cares for me. It can physically make me tingle with anticipation and overflow with desire to do the same for her."

"I'm a romantic guy," said a screenwriter from Los Angeles. "When I'm in a committed relationship and I feel unconditional love, I like sending cards; I like sending flowers. I like doing tiny, seemingly insignificant things that I know will mean something to the woman I love. I believe doing those things sustains the love. But I've been through two divorces and I know enough at fifty-four years old to understand it takes two. If one person makes all the effort and the other person seldom responds, romance is dead."

"I need a reason to want to do those things for a woman," said Joshua a thirty-two year old community hospital admitting clerk. "If someone is constantly measuring what I do or don't do, or is constantly harping at me for every indiscretion, I just don't feel like making any extra effort."

"I remember it like it was yesterday," said a forty-seven year old real estate developer from Florida. "Even after ten years of being divorced, the wound opens just by thinking about it. I remember my ex-wife used to complain bitterly that I never bought her anything personal. I was raised with brothers and a tyrannical father. I don't really know what women like. Sure, I gave flowers and perfume to her over the years but she was always complaining that this one's husband bought her a beautiful nightgown, or that one's husband bought her the perfect necklace. Try as I might, nothing I seemed to buy was ever any good. One day I was passing this little boutique in town and they happened to be dressing the window. They had just draped the mannequin in what I thought was the most beautiful bathrobe I had ever seen, and I'm not the kind of guy who really notices this stuff. It was a soft, super fluffy fabric in a cool, turquoise color with an Indian motif piping. It was $100 but I thought it was perfect and worth it. I kept it at my office for almost three months before our anniversary. Every time I even looked at the package, I felt excited. This time she'll be thrilled, I thought. I almost couldn't wait to give it to her. When I did, she looked at me after opening the box and said it was nice but *the fabric was too heavy for our climate.* Right then, something drained right out of me. Romance?" he asked, "How can you *want* to be romantic or buy little things for someone who's always finding fault with any decision you make?"

"When I brought flowers home for no reason," said a fifty year old textile executive, "my ex-wife would chastise me for spending too much money. Chocolates at Valentine's Day would cause her to gain weight. My taste in clothes made my company thousands of dollars, but in her eyes nothing I chose for her had any merit. After twenty-four years of marriage to someone like that, you start to think, *Is this all there is?* Now I'm with a gal that thanks me if I bring her a pack of gum. She was married twenty years to a husband that never made any effort, *ever.* He'd sign his name to a card but he never did anything special. Marcia appreciates everything I do and that appreciation is why I do something and think of her every chance I get. I walked in with a bottle of *Crystal* last Friday night, just because we had been watching "Lifestyles of the Rich and Famous" the week before and she saw the champagne on TV wondering aloud what it could possibly taste like to cost $100 a bottle. She almost cried when I handed it to her as a surprise. I'm fifty years old but with Marcia I feel like a high schooler in heat. I love doing things for her."

From the vast cross section of men I've interviewed and the data I've collected, men unquestionably want and require romance in their lives. In fact, many modern men daydream about it the same way we do. It may not be the central focus of their lives, but it surely is something they miss if denied. Some men are just better at *being* romantic than others, but men tell me relentlessly, that if rebuffed, they *bury* their need to demonstrate love.

"I've been with enough women," offered Jake, a forty-three

year old machinist from Grand Rapids, Michigan, "to know that women need to feel in love to make love. I've tried to do things to show how much I care, but I'm not always smooth the way some fellas are, so I'm self-conscious about it. When I do make the effort, if I'm laughed at or chastened in any way, I freeze. I want to run, and a little something dies in me. It takes me a long time to initiate something for that woman again. I'll respond when she makes the effort, but I become insecure about sticking my neck out again."

When men feel hurt, unsure, unloved, or more commonly, unappreciated, they lose their desire to *demonstrate* their affection. The tender places in a man's heart and psyche are reaffirmed when he falls in love, but a lifetime of defenses established to prevent his emotions from coming to the surface emerge. He becomes locked in a battle of taking down a wall and putting it back up. When he does lower the wall, if he's continuously rebuffed, he begins to let it down less and less. In order to have a man lower his wall and become more adventurous romantically, he has to feel loved, and a man feels most loved when he's appreciated and *valued*. He needs to know he matters. We all have a need to know we matter. We certainly don't respond when someone falls all over us, but we all have a need to have our opinion valued, our self-worth confirmed, and our desirability acknowledged. When we devalue a gesture or a gift we begin to set up a chain reaction of hurt and confusion within our relationships. He becomes alienated and won't buy us anything other than a toaster. We take that as a sign: *he made no effort, therefore he doesn't care*. This wounds us and we belittle the way he drives, combs his hair or dresses. On and on it goes, and where it stops, nobody knows.

But we do know where it stops, it usually stops at divorce court or worse—the prison of being involved in unloving relationships.

It is within our control to keep that from happening, but it takes great patience and great effort. If we want fulfilling relationships, like the ones we imagine, then we must take responsibility for our own happiness. If we want romance in our lives, we must give the man in our life a reason to *be* romantic. We must give him a reason to act that way.

You can scream at me all you want about what comes first, the chicken or the egg, but again my answer is, who cares? If you as a woman have the capacity and ability to create sustained happiness for yourself and your partner, isn't accomplishing it what counts? Isn't it time we stop worrying about who does what and simply enjoy the results?

I accept and understand that it is much easier for me to embrace the emotions needed to *initiate* romance than it is for most men to do the same. Women's socialization geared us in that direction. We are comfortable moving in and out of the daily emotional dramas of friends and family, and we nurture, give support, and listen almost on demand. We seldom have to stop and think about our responses, they just come naturally. Men are becoming more fluent in emotional responses, but they lag behind us in that area, needing to stop, think, and then effect the appropriate response. That's why he may not always recognize our genuine attempts to ignite the flames and why he generally isn't as creative at igniting them as we are.

When he doesn't make the attempt, or recognize our attempt, we read that as rejection, or his self-absorption or out-and-out coldness. We then become hurt and reactive, and in some cases it's warranted. Indeed, there are those men who do appear callous and indifferent. Deep down, I believe all men genuinely want to be loved and to show love. But some bury their needs deeper than others. Some we can reach, others we cannot. Again, it's an educated decision whether or not to pursue someone who doesn't show you the love you need. Can you live with the lack of romance? Can you do what's required to rekindle it or to keep it from ever waning? Are you the kind of person who can willingly make the necessary effort? Or should you legitimately walk away, just like the fifty year old textile executive who finally realized that with some people, the expenditure will *never* guarantee a return?

The good news is that most loving people do react; most

loving people do not want to live in hollow, meaningless relationships, and most loving people will respond, in spite of their previous hurt and fear—*if we care enough to find and push the right buttons.*

I hate to oversimplify, but when a child draws a picture for you and you praise the colors and how well they executed it, they visibly brighten and want to run right back and make another for you. It's almost exactly the same with men. If you demonstrate your love, you cause them to show theirs in return. If you don't show anger when your gestures are rebuffed, therefore exacerbating the negative, and you give love again... and even again as needed, it *will* eventually flow back to you. (From a basically healthy, well-adjusted person)

But that's hard for most of us, to be rebuffed and still give love again without reacting or striking back in anger.

This chapter supplies the tools necessary to understand what men say they need to become more loving, and therefore, more romantic and then, how to apply them, if you choose. But just like the horse you lead to water, you cannot *make* her drink. Some readers may choose not to make the effort, content to pine for what they don't have. Some may resent having to initiate the effort, resigning themselves to accept what they lack, and others will reevaluate their position, wanting to promulgate and intensify everlasting love, sustained happiness, and on-going passion.

For me, there is no contest.

WHAT ROMANCE ISN'T

Before undertaking the effort necessary to create an everlasting love, one must have realistic expectations of it. We must come to the realization that no love can assuage all hurt. No love can insulate us from fear and disappointment. No love can shield us from anger. No love is *perfect* and neither are lovers. There are no guarantees in life. No guarantees that those we love, will return that love or treat us right, and no guarantees our actions can influence every situation.

The only guarantee we have is knowing that if what we've

been doing in the past is not making us happy, we must learn to alter it until it does. We must rebuild the foundation if it no longer supports the structure, and for many of us, that's much more difficult than it sounds.

Jason, a fifty-one year old contractor clearly remembers the day life as *he* knew it came to a screeching halt. "With a six year-old and a nine year-old, I worked hard but made good money. My wife Nancy was thirty-nine then. We had two nice cars, a great house, money in the bank and traditional roles. I thought everything was great. Everything had gone according to a plan that seemed preordained. On that day ten years ago, eleven years into our marriage, Nancy confronted me with her discontent. She told me that it wasn't that she was unhappy in the marriage or with the kids or even the roles. She said she was no longer comfortable with *me*.

"At first I chalked it up to the old standby—PMS. But it was obvious it had no connection to water weight gain. This was serious, and Nancy was more serious than I'd ever seen her. She wasn't ranting and she wasn't raving. She was ascetically explaining that if I wanted the relationship to continue, I'd have to hear her out, think about what she was saying, and I'd have to *change*. Those are words that can cut any man to the quick faster than a sword- wielding dervish. But this was something that really wasn't funny. Nancy was dead serious and her concerns rocked the very foundation of our marriage. When I realized it wasn't a mood swing or something that would go away, I had to take a long, hard look at what she was saying, which was hard for a guy like me. I don't like being told things. But I also wasn't willing to lose her and the life we built either. And frankly, when I listened to what she was stoically but clearly telling me, I couldn't disagree. We were indeed going through all the motions. We made love, we played tennis together, we went on vacations, played with the kids and parented together. We did everything right. We did everything *together* yet somehow we were drifting further and further away from the love we once shared, and yet we both still really loved each other. It just somehow was disappearing more and more each year and I didn't understand why; apparently, Nancy did.

"I sulked for days. I ignored it for a few more, then I realized that deep down in the recesses of my heart, I was missing that spark, that passion and I guess that *romance* as much as she was. I just buried my need for it in other ways, mostly working until I became numb.

"She was right, it was a great life but one that was becoming devoid of any passion. So, as much for me as for her, I decided to change. I made a conscious decision to adjust how I did things and reacted to things. I did not place all the burden on my wife. It wasn't always easy, but now looking back, I was just as dead inside as she was. I wondered how I could have let it happen. How could I shut down from a part of my life that is so important to the very quality of how I'm living it?"

Today, with their kids almost grown, Nancy and Jason still look like newlyweds. They prefer each other's company to almost anyone else's. They laugh, are incredibly playful, and they still have a passion for each other that is the envy of most of their friends... and the *center* of their relationship. What happened? They sat down and calmly and intelligently discussed the importance of putting romance back into their lives, and exactly how to do just that. Jason had to make himself less self-absorbed. No matter how busy at work he thought he was, no matter how heavy a load he thought he had to carry, he had to willingly, not begrudgingly, but *willingly* set aside time to be with Nancy, and Nancy alone. He couldn't make her ask for it or beg for it, he had to lovingly provide it. And he couldn't be half there and still half in his office. She in turn had to understand that every romantic attempt she made could not be reciprocated. The timing had to be right for both of them, and when it wasn't returned, she would not take it personally. She would not react to it as though it were rejection. She would not get angry and retaliate. She would simply express her disappointment, reaffirm her love and understanding and simply trust that Jason *would* respond. "And I did," he said. "I couldn't always meet her needs when she needed them met, but now I knew when she had needs. Now I put her on an equal par with my work, with watching sports, with everything that used to come first. I gave our life together equal importance. Now, instead of being at the office until eleven every night or every weekend, I set aside prearranged time just for her. Actually, just for us. I made dates with her. I planned surprises. I took her out and I spontaneously called on the spur of the moment. *And I responded when she made overtures to me.* I think that meant the most to her, that I opened myself enough to respond and appreciate her efforts.

"She isn't always in the mood to meet my needs either, but we've struck a balance and when our individual needs aren't met by the other, neither of us gets hurt and angry anymore. The difference is that now we just understand that our lives are hectic and when we can steal time, we do. We don't bury the anger or resentment anymore, we discuss it. I know that Nancy is more loving towards me because she doesn't constantly have to ask or fight for my attention and she isn't continually being rejected. I didn't realize how that must have made her feel inside. I didn't realize that in little insignificant ways she was purposefully trying to hurt me in return. I'd react to that, and a whole progression of anger and resentment was created that never really abated.

"Having my loving wife back in my corner; caring enough for each other to do special things, making love because we're in love rather than just extracting sexual release is something now regained, I'll never let go of again. I didn't realize how empty my *full* life was until I got it back."

No one can be all things to another person. We must indeed keep our separate identities for our self-esteem to flourish. However, we cannot keep ourselves so separate that we don't remember why we fell in love in the first place. There is no lonelier feeling than living within a relationship that has died. We're becoming a society of the walking wounded, devoid of the intense pleasures of living, loving and growing old with someone you still desire. Love is the most precious of all gifts, the most valuable of all possessions, and it is the most enduring IF it is nurtured and nourished, for that is the only way it will grow and deepen. The same is true of love's soulmate—romance. Romance is not something that just happens because you want it to. It's something you make happen if you care to.

Or it's something, you don't.

Chapter 21

Love Is The Answer -
How To Keep The Bonfires Burning ...Forever

"'Clink' go the Baccarat wine glasses as he gazes into my eyes. With candles flickering and soft music in the background, he gets up, sweeps me into his arms and we dance, locked in each other's tight embrace," says Candace, a forty year old office manager. "Of course, this is my dream, and in it, I'm twenty pounds lighter, wearing a sexy black Dior original and dripping in about forty grand worth of Bulgari jewels," she laughs.

This may be the stuff that lurks in the souls of Danielle Steel and Barbara Cartwright, but of few men who are still breathing. If we want romance in our lives we must have the courage to initiate it. We must understand how to create it and how to keep it alive once we do, and we must understand that in most cases we are going to be much better at creating romance, than the man we want to create it with. We must also be accepting and appreciative of the romantic gestures that are sent our direction, even if they are not exactly what we had in mind.

"Oh yes, I'm romantic," says a handsome twenty-eight year old actor. "I do cards and flowers."

"He wouldn't know romance if it got up and bit him in the butt," retorts his twenty-six year old, ex live-in lover. Granted, romance is surely in the eye of the beholder, but a balance struck between a man's and a woman's perceptions, can be the difference in a relationship that has the power to last and one that merely flickers and dies.

In *The Bridges Of Madison County*, a short, simple book that reigned on the best seller list over a year, the character of Francesca had a wondrous romantic four day interlude with a veritable stranger who left her life as swiftly as he had entered it. But still, after twenty-seven years, the thought of him, the feel of him, and the memory of those four days with him were as real and as powerful to her as if they had happened yesterday. Romance and the passion it creates has the capacity to make someone *feel special*. That, in itself, is one of the most powerful aphrodisiacs known to man. The bonus is, that its effect is equally as powerful for the giver as it is for the recipient.

And often, the simplest expression leaves the most lasting impression. It doesn't take much effort to send a card to someone you care about, or to bring a flower home, or to stop for just two minutes out of a busy day to call and say, "I can't talk, but I just wanted you to know I love you," to get up extra early and make a surprise breakfast in bed, or to stop and bring home his or her favorite wine, or ice cream. "I give my girlfriend little gift certificates," offers a thirty-eight year old father of four. "With our jobs, her kids, my kids, it's hard to find time in our regular routine to be romantic, let alone think of ways to carry them out. So, I just bought these inexpensive little blank certificates. Then, when I think of things I'd like us to have the time to do together I fill one out, and leave it on her pillow, or mail one to her." Jane, his harried thirty-seven year old lover says, "I think that's why I love him so, he makes me feel cherished. Even with all the hustle and bustle of our lives, he still thinks of me. I know he loves me, but it means so much more to be shown every so often."

There are a thousand ways—little, inexpensive, uncomplicated ways, to let someone who's important to you, know that you care. What was the most romantic thing you ever did for anybody? And what was the most romantic thing anyone ever did for you? This chapter highlights some of the more creative and interesting responses men offered. Plus, it demonstrates how easy it can be to ignite your own blaze by listing more than fifty suggestions for the romantic neophyte, guaranteed to start the sparks flying.

The importance of romance might well be the best of all lessons learned about love and happiness, for there is no greater power, nor greater joy than taking the time to show someone, "I care!"

"The most romantic thing I ever did," said thirty-nine year old John, a physical therapist from Spokane, Washington "was my death-by-chocolate night. I knew the woman I was dating was a chocolate freak, so I invited her over for dinner and filled my apartment with everything chocolate. I served her a two pound chocolate kiss on a platter. I had chocolate roses in the center of the table. I had a chocolate souffle made by a local restaurant for the main course. Chocolate dipped strawberries for dessert, and I had a jar of the most decadent chocolate sauce, which we used rather creatively, later in the evening! I think I enjoyed *preparing* it all as much as I enjoyed her reaction to seeing it. When you love someone, just the effort gives you pleasure. If you get a positive reaction, it's *magic*."

"The most romantic thing I ever did," said a forty-one year old periodontist from Witchita, Kansas "was after arriving in New York for a three day conference. I called home and my girlfriend sounded so lonely. I realized how much she loved me *after* I went away. During the call I heard our local radio station playing their nighttime love songs in the background. I remembered they took dedications, so I called information, got their number and they played "The Look of Love," and recorded my voice asking her to marry me over the radio. It took her twenty minutes to call me to say, 'yes'—she was crying so hard she kept dialing wrong numbers."

"My shining romantic moment was the night I kidnaped my wife," exclaimed a forty-four year old photographer from Lowell, Massachusetts. "I called her mom and begged her to babysit our three rug rats for the weekend. When mom rang the bell to report for duty, I was right behind her with a satin blindfold, a gardenia corsage (just like the one I bought her on our first date) and a limo waiting in the driveway. My wife was dumbfounded as I removed the dishtowel from her shoulder, pinned on the corsage and whisked her away. We had fabulous food, a fabulous room and made memories that have lasted a lifetime. I realized, what are we killing ourselves for if we lose each other in the process?"

"I knew my girlfriend and I were at a difficult point in our relationship," said a thirty-one year old maintenance contractor from Shreveport, Louisiana. It's not easy for me to show my feelings or express my love, and although I knew she really loved me, I could sense she was coming to the end of her patience, and I didn't want to lose her. I had just read something in the newspaper about romance, and it got me thinking. *How hard could it be*, I asked myself. I called her at her office, and told her not to ask the eighty million questions she'd normally ask, when I tell her to go home after work and get decked out to the nines. I said she'd receive further instructions when she got there. Since I always got home two hours ahead of her, I left a pitcher of freshly made pina coladas, which I hate but which she loves, in the fridge and a little red shopping bag on the counter which contained a bottle of expensive bubble bath and perfume, along with a note that told her to pour herself a drink, take a luxurious bath and to be ready promptly at 7:15.

"I borrowed my buddy's Mercedes for the night (we both drive Nissans); I got dressed at his house, and at 7:15 sharp, I called for her. When she answered the door, she looked so beautiful and happy, that she almost took my breath away. I gave her a rose and we kissed so long and hard we almost didn't get out the door. I took her to a restaurant she had been hinting about for four years! We held hands; she cried a little and we had a great bottle of wine and a dinner that was spectacular. On the ride home, she sat next to me and I fondled her like when we first met. The electricity, desire and love surging through my body and hers made me stop for a minute to think, if it could be like this, if just this little bit of effort could restore this intensity, why in the world did it take me so long to realize it? And why did I resist it? I don't always have the money for exactly that kind of night, but now I actually get pleasure from dreaming up others, even seemingly insignificant ideas. Not only hadn't I realized how much finally showing this kind of affection would mean to her, I never would have believed how much the intensity of that night impacted *me*."

"The most romantic thing anyone ever did for me," responded a twenty-nine year old cosmetic dentist from Newark, Delaware, "was to open my eyes. I always thought those romantic Fabio-types were soupy, soapy wimps that really only turned a woman on for one thing and one thing only. Then my girlfriend slapped me into reality. I'm your more pragmatic kind of guy. Nothing fancy, no frills. On my birthday, she made me a card that said for this whole day I was going to be given present after present that will allow me to release what she called my antiquated inhibitions... and there was a stern P.S.—that if I didn't go along, that if I caused my usual fuss or put up my usual resistance, she'd be packed and out the door before I got one day older.

"That was my first awakening, knowing I was not going to control this situation. The next thing she did was to make me this fabulous bath. I don't think I had taken a bath since I was a kid. She filled the tub with apricot bubbles, she moved the TV into the room and gave me the remote control along with a rather strong Screwdriver and some freshly cut fruit along with muffins on a tubside tray. My mind started to object, but something told me to just give in and enjoy it. Next, came a terrific breakfast omelet she arranged on our patio. As if on cue with my last bite, the doorbell rang and in walked a big Russian masseuse named Ivan. I swear, he was so big that if I thought about objecting, it went right out of my head. I was treated to fifty-five minutes of sheer heaven. You know, I never had a massage before.

"After about a three hour nap, I was awakened by soft

music and soft red lights. She had removed the light bulbs in our bedroom and replaced them with red bulbs. When she walked in, my eyes nearly bulged out of my head. She had on garters, high heels and a short satin nightshirt that left little to the imagination. Needless to say, my whole body started to throb. She brought in a bottle of champagne and for the rest of the day-into-night we alternated between making love, eating, and watching movies. It was the best birthday, and the wake-up call I needed. I don't know what I was afraid of or why I seldom let myself go like that. All I know is, that once a month or so we treat ourselves to that kind of day. I used to fight it, even criticize her for wanting it. Now I realize it's what our relationship needed to revitalize itself. I'm still not the greatest at initiating that stuff on my own, but I have brought some dandy things home to contribute."

"The most romantic thing anyone ever did for me," said a twenty-nine year old former professional baseball player, "was telling me to get in, sit down and shut up. My girlfriend whisked me away on a Friday afternoon just as I was parking in my condo's garage. She already had packed for us, and about four hours later we pulled up to a little lodge right on Lake Winnepesaukee in New Hampshire. We picnicked in the car while *she* drove the whole way. At first I wanted to put up a fight, but when I realized how much effort she made, and how she seemed to need to do this, I just gave into it. I'm sure glad I did. It was exactly what I needed, and what the relationship needed... some quiet, uninterrupted, romantic down-time. The whole three days were wonderful. We walked, talked, fished, ate and remembered why we got together in the first place. The hustle and bustle of life can really take its toll; I don't know if we realize how much of a toll, until it's too late. I asked her to marry me that weekend and we promised each other that if either of us got too crazy or too caught up in life, to the detriment of our relationship, we'd kidnap the other and come right back to New Hampshire."

Romance won't just perpetuate itself, we have to work at it

as diligently as we work at anything that matters to us. Sometimes men need a push. Sometimes their own efforts just need to be appreciated. Whatever the case, the end result is that making the time is worth the effort. If we care enough to fall in love with someone, we should care enough to keep that love alive, and doing so may only require a creative jump start. A conversation where you both agree to spend some time together and agree during that time to bite your tongues if anything goes wrong. Make your lover promise not to deck the hotel clerk if the right room isn't ready. You promise not to comment on the salt in the food or how much the wine costs. He vows not to get hysterical if you get caught in traffic on the way, or if he can't find a parking spot. Agree to spend some romantic time together free from judgments and recriminations. Just indulge, enjoy and make the effort needed to see each other as the person you fell in love with now... and always.

SOME IDEAS TO IGNITE EVEN THE ROMANTIC NEOPHYTE

When asked what a woman had ever done to make them *feel* romantic, many of the men interviewed came up with some pretty incredible ideas and stories of their own. After sorting the outlandish from the ordinary and everything in between, this list of twenty-five should get anyone's motor revving. And as if that weren't enough, there's a list of twenty-five more suggestions that hopefully will give you some additional inspiration.

1/ "When a woman kisses me for no reason. Especially if it's one of those deep passionate ones."

2/ "If a woman who's sitting across from me opens my palm, and gently kisses or licks it as she looks into my eyes, it drives me wild with desire."

3/ "I once woke up to a white envelope with a lipstick print on it. Inside was yet another print on a note that said, *Until*

Tonight. After I got up, I found about *400 more* prints of her lips in bright red lipstick pasted all over my apartment. On my glasses, on my toothbrush, on my fish tank, in my cabinets. I even found one on each of the first six pieces of toilet paper I unrolled! Boy, was that a decadent feeling. I went out and bought her every sexy thing I could find to bring home that night. I couldn't even concentrate at work. I just kept seeing those lips!"

4/ "I remember coming home from a really lousy day at the office, and as I was walking up my path to the house, I saw all these chocolate Kisses sort of leading the way. At first, I was almost annoyed. *Oh great! someone spilled chocolate all over my walkway and tomorrow there'll be an army of ants.* Then I realized my wife had done it. When I stopped to get the mail, there was one of those big Kisses in the mailbox. When I opened the front door her skirt was just suspended on a cord from the chandelier. At first I thought, *What the hell is going on here?* Up the first few stairs I saw her blouse thrown on the railing. Up a few more stairs her pantyhose just laid there. Now I finally got it. On the top of the landing her bra hit me in the face, with quite the dab of perfume. A few more steps into our bedroom found her sitting wrapped in aluminum foil with a white streamer coming out of the top. It said, *Unwrap me for a sweet sensation*. Needless to say the rest of the horrible day was forgotten. It was just what I needed."

5/ "The most romantic thing to me is to make love in front of a fire. I came home during a snow storm all tense, and when I walked in, she had soft music playing and two huge fluffy comforters on the floor in front of the fire. She handed me a glass of wine along with a tray of hors'doeuvres and we unwound together in front of a roaring fire."

6/ "About 4pm on a Friday afternoon my secretary walked into my office carrying this huge, elaborately wrapped carton. The accompanying note said "If you want to have the night of your life, bring this package and meet me at 6:30 sharp at Pelican's Point. Inside the box was a delight for every sense: a can of pâté and crackers for taste, a sexy negligee for sight, a Luther Vandross tape for hearing, incense for smell and a double size feather bed with a satin cover for touch. My heart started to race and my face flushed. I know my secretary was chuckling as she left my office.

"Since it was late September and already pretty cold, there was no one else there. My wife had set up a heater, our son's small pop-up tent and fluffy sleeping bags on which we put the feather bed. No one had every really gone out of their way for me like this before. What an incredibly electric feeling to be making love in such a public, yet private spot. For weeks later I couldn't stop thinking about that night... and my wife."

7/ "I got a FedEx about noon on Friday from my girlfriend. Inside the package was a sexy satin bra, matching panties and a lightly perfumed note that read – *Informal modeling – 6pm, my place*. I got shivers and had to stay seated all day."

8/ "I got home about 6pm one night and although my girlfriend's car was in the driveway, no one answered when I called out, but since it's a three level house, I just thought no one had heard me. We live with her son and he wasn't home either. When I got up the stairs there was this huge gift-wrapped box in the living room with a huge bow. The note said, *Tom, this is the most precious gift I could give you*. I went to move the box but I barely could. So I lifted off the lid. There was my girlfriend in a black bra, black fish net hose and black underwear lying on a red satin sheet with a red satin pillow under her head. She had the most incredible grin on her face! What a surprise."

9/ "When I drove up my street I noticed a red glow where I thought my house was. As I got closer I realized our white outdoor lights had been replaced by red bulbs. In fact, the one by the front door was blinking! I couldn't imagine what was going on. As I got to the front door I saw a huge black X on it. Inside the door there were three more black Xs taped to the wall, illuminated only by a small night light that also now had a red bulb. Other than that, the house was pitch black. I walked up the stairs, and in the hallway was a chair and a note that said,

Show starts in two minutes. Take a seat. I started to grin from ear to ear. Strip tease music started to play, and out from behind a black tablecloth hung in the doorway to resemble a curtain, stepped my girlfriend in a frilly outfit, complete with a boa and a fan made of feathers. She stepped onto her Jane Fonda step exerciser which acted like a platform and she proceeded to do the most incredible strip tease just for me. Talk about romance. I couldn't get her out of my mind for months."

10/ "When I got to work I stopped at my secretary's desk to give her a report I needed typed. When I opened my briefcase there was a pair of underwear my girlfriend had obviously slipped in before I left, along with a note that announced: *Tonight's the night!*"

11/ "Do you have any idea the tingle I got when I opened a box that was sent by courier to my office only to find a naked Barbie doll inside? The note said, *I'll show you mine if you show me yours!!!*"

12/ "When I came home I saw a little box that someone had left in front of my door. I took it in and opened it. There was a doll inside. It had three big labels that covered all three private parts. Each was marked 1, 2 or 3. The note said, *Pull tab 1*. I did, nothing happened. Then the note said *Pull tab 2*. I did, still nothing happened. Finally the note said *Pull tab 3*. Under tab 3 was a tiny note that said *See how easy that was? Practice can make perfect. Making love to me can be as easy as 1,2,3 or maybe not. See you at eight.* I broke out into a cold sweat. How clever, how imaginative... how titillating!

13/ "One Halloween I came home to find a note on the door that said, *In the living room you'll find a trick and a treat.* There sat my girlfriend in the middle of the rug on top of leaves she had strewn around wearing nothing but an orange sheet. She was my Halloween pumpkin."

14/ "For my birthday, my wife bought me a beautiful watch and engraved on the back was—*I'll always have time for you, I just need you to make time for me.*"

15/ "When I stopped at the Post Office to pick up my mail, there was a note that said they had a box too large to fit, waiting for me at the desk. When I picked it up, it piqued my curiosity, so I opened it in the car. Inside was an old-fashioned alarm clock with a note that said, *I'm broken-hearted that we haven't found time for each other lately. I miss you!* I drove right over to my girlfriend's house, but I stopped to pick up wine and flowers first. She got my attention."

16/ "I got a clock along with a note that said, *If you want the time of your life call* _____ and it gave my girlfriend's number. I couldn't wait to hear her voice. Boy, did that make me feel wanted."

17/ "My wife and I had been so busy, it seemed like we never had time to make love anymore. When I got to work I reached into my jacket pocket for something and found a piece of folded paper on which my wife wrote Webster's definition of orgasm! On the back she wrote: *If you want to remember how it feels, meet me in your parking lot at 6pm.* She drove up wearing nothing but a raincoat."

18/ "When I got to my car after work, I saw a single red rose on the windshield. Thinking someone must have left it on the wrong car, I got in and decided I'd surprise my girlfriend with it. As soon as I turned on the ignition, out of the tape player came her voice detailing the kind of night I could have if I got myself over to her place, pronto. The longer she talked, the more I started to sweat with anticipation."

19/ "I use a Dictaphone machine to record my thoughts and ideas or letters I need to write. One day I pushed the "On" button to play back what I had last recorded and out pops the sound of my girlfriend's voice telling me what she was planning for our next encounter. I was grateful I was in my office, not on a plane. It was such a surprise. It made me feel incredibly erotic."

20/ "To me, anything with candles, incense and soft-music can get me into a romantic mood. The more candles the better. As soon as I see them, there's no difficulty in setting the mood."

21/ "I think the most romantic times are the unplanned, whole day affairs. It could start out by just running errands together, stopping at a quaint little place for lunch sharing a bottle of wine, and great conversation. Walking somewhere hand in hand. Those are the times that are real romantic to me."

22/ "For my birthday I received a box that was beautifully wrapped. Inside was a silver cardboard crown and a note that read: *By a close margin you have been elected King for a Night. This is the evening you will be pampered and pleasured beyond your wildest dreams. The games begin at 7pm sharp—your place.*"

23/ "My girlfriend was always complaining that I was obsessive about reading the newspaper. One day when I got home there was a note with letters cut from the newspaper that read: *All the news that's fit to read you'll find upstairs behind door number #1.* When I got to our bedroom there was a huge #1 on the door. I walked in and couldn't believe my eyes; she had covered the drapes, the bed and the bureaus with newspaper, and there she sat in the middle with two thin bands of newspaper covering her private parts. She held a note that read: *C-O-M-E, read all about it.* I laughed so hard, I just about died. She had gone to such trouble—what a wonderful way to get her point across."

24/ "Boy, was I surprised when I got a VCR tape in the mail. No note, no return address. When I popped it in to watch it, I couldn't believe it. My wife, who was away for the week, made me the most sensuous tape I'd ever seen. First she read me a beautiful poem. She threw me kisses. She edited in clips of some X-rated movies and then finished with a little strip tease of her own, but she stopped just before the good parts. She said that to see those, I'd have to wait until she got home. I surprised her. The night before she was to return home, I showed up at the hotel with champagne and uncontrollable desire! We had the best three days ever."

25/ "Breakfast in bed was something I had read about and always thought about, but at thirty-seven, no one had ever done for me. I had done it for some women in my life, but I never had the pleasure, until my girlfriend came in one day with everything from fresh brewed coffee to fresh fruits, and muffins she had gotten up early to make. It felt so good to be cared for like that."

TWENTY-FIVE MORE CREATIVE IDEAS TO BURN THE BARN TO THE GROUND.
YOU CAN USE THEM AS IS OR COME UP WITH CREATIVE DERIVATIVES OF YOUR OWN.

1/ Send him on a love hunt. Leave little messages at different spots that give him instructions or clues to get him to the next spot. You can do this in your own house and have him running all around to find you or send him to the liquor store to pick-up wine you've already prepaid and left there. Attached to the bottle should be a note telling him to drive to the record store for a prepaid tape of his favorite sexy artist on which you've written the name of the hotel or destination you're waiting at. This just adds a little spice.

2/ Make breakfast in bed. Almost any day will start out romantic if it begins by making someone feel special. Heart shaped pancakes. Or pancakes that spell: I love you. Even jam on an English muffin could be in a heart. You can make little flags from tiny notes you've glued on toothpicks. There are so many ideas that just take a few minutes, but that create memories that will last a lifetime.

3/ Send something sexy to his place of business, in a box, in an envelope or in a balloon. There are hundreds of creative ideas that will start his blood boiling, especially if he's not expecting it.

4/ Give him gift certificates for a night as his love slave... or his French maid or whatever you think his fantasy might be.

5/ Stick a sexy, sweet note into his jacket pocket, his lunch or his briefcase. Be creative. Invite him to a private dinner, a bubble bath or his fantasy. Every time he pulls the note out, he won't be able to stop thinking of you.

6/ Kidnap him. Make all the arrangements you need to set it up in advance. Then show up at his office and whisk him away. You can kidnap him for a night or a whole weekend.

7/ Charter a boat for a few hours, just for the two of you.

8/ Splurge on a bottle of good champagne and all different sized white candles. Scatter them around your bedroom and light them near the time when he's expected home. A few sticks of incense strategically placed around the room also helps to set the mood. There will be no need for words.

9/ Make a book for him. Punch holes in several 5 1/2 x 8 1/2 inch paper and thread a ribbon or gold cord through the holes. Write him a sexy poem. Paste a picture of yourself. Cut out some romantic scenes. Tell him what you want to do to him. Or make a booklet of personal gift certificates.

10/ Show up at his office for lunch or after work in just a rain coat. Try to get an elevator for just the two of you. Flash him.

Just make sure he's not driving when you do!

11/ Buy ten pair of extremely sexy satin underwear in different colors and stick them all over the house while he's sleeping, each with a different message. Or put one in his briefcase, one in his car, one in his coat pocket and so on.

12/ Hire a limo. The possibilities here are endless. And if it's an experience the two of you have never shared, it's money well spent for an incredible evening. Most limousines cost only thirty to fifty dollars per hour, usually with a three hour limit.

13/ Make him an audio tape and talk softly and sexy as if you're whispering in his ear.

14/ Buy him a basketful of exotic smelling massage oils accompanied by personal gift certificate entitling him to the most sensuous massage he's ever had.

15/ Dress yourself up as something. Rent a costume or make one. The candy Kiss—made from aluminum foil and a streamer of white paper for the note, is the easiest and sometimes the most effective, but there are hundreds of possibilities.

16/ If you're so inclined, make reservations at an X-rated motel. Or splurge and book a trip to the Poconos where they have heart shaped hot tubs, round beds and enough satin to qualify for a sultan's bounty. Or rent an X-rated tape and watch it together.

17/ Plan a very romantic morning or evening for no special reason. Hire someone to clean just before, so you don't feel compelled to straighten up. Take the phone off the hook, and indulge each other. Order in your favorite foods, make it a decadent time that fulfills all the things you say you're going to do, but never get time for.

18/ Offer to play strip poker.

19/ Plan to make love in a different location, not just the bedroom. Invest in a luxurious down filled comforter or feather bed and put it in another room surrounded by candles and play soft music in the background.

20/ Buy an expensive set of luxurious satin sheets, and turn up the A/C. Make the room a little chilly (even in summer!) and snuggle under a big fluffy comforter.

21/ Send him a scroll with an itinerary numbered one through ten. At one just write: *spend the whole day (Saturday) with you doing exactly what you want*. Include a pen and tell him to fill in the rest.

22/ Have him sit down with his favorite wine or other beverage and give him ten little boxes. Inside each would be one of the reasons you love him or are turned on by him. (Or ten things you want to do to him)

23/ If he's a visual guy, treat yourself to the outfit you believe he'd find the sexiest on you, and wear it out of the blue when he walks in the door. Men are very visual and nothing turns them on more than by seeing someone they love, looking exceptional.

24/ Kiss him every morning and remind him why you love him.

25/ Use your infinite wisdom and imagination to keep your love alive. There are so many ways to add spice to your life. So many little gestures you can make to rekindle the sparks that are so vital to the health of your relationship. Don't be shy, don't be timid and don't stand on ceremony. If you try something and it doesn't work the first time, don't get angry, or hurt, just try again. Some men who have been emotionally deprived or whom I call *romantically challenged*, need a little coaxing. Figuring out how to keep your love exciting is the most important contribution you can make to it.

LOVE IS THE ANSWER

Love and all its glory is the most potent of all emotions. Love is exalted joy, a permeating passion from the depths of our souls. Love is the feeling of being completely one with another. It inspires us, it confirms us, and it sets us free. It is pleasure and comfort and a sense of peace that is inexplicable – an emotion so powerful, it involves all our senses at once.

But when love is lost, it is a searing pain, a despair and sense of loneliness that cuts us to the core.

Alfred Lord Tennyson said, "...'Tis better to have loved and lost than never to have loved at all." I'm not quite sure I agree with him. If you don't know what you're missing, you won't feel the depth of its loss when it's gone. Living within a relationship where love has come and gone has got to be one of the loneliest experiences on earth. Thinking back to the joys, to the hopes, and to the expectations you both had when you were in love, and wondering what went wrong, is sheer unadulterated misery.

If you've ever felt that way, then you must know that keeping love alive once you've found it, is a prize without equal and the greatest gift you can bestow on the one you profess to love. It is still possible even in our hurry-up world, if you make the decision that no matter what other goals you set, what other rewards you seek or what other priorities you develop, that you will never lose sight of the one you love and never forget what that love means to you. Because if you do, you do so consciously knowing that you may lose the thing you once prized most.

And you may not be able to get it back.

Love does indeed make the world go round. And the only ally with the power to restore love and fuel it – is romance.

If MEN: The Handbook gives you just one thing, let it give you *the desire and willingness* to seize the information provided herein and the freedom to be able to utilize it.

EPILOGUE

This book was written to promote better understanding between the sexes and to keep us from accessing blame. It was written so that women will have better comprehension of how a man thinks, and therefore why he reacts as he does.

Changing partners and blindly going from relationship to relationship in search of happiness can't possibly be the way to find it.

Understanding each other, loving each other free from conditions, showing tenderness and compassion, and treating our partners with the same kindnesses and respect we give virtual strangers, has got to be the answer to sustained happiness.

And treating others as we ourselves wish to be treated, is the only place to begin.